Belonging

Poetry of Diaspora in Silicon Valley

Dr. Jyoti Bachani, Editor

Being | Becoming | Belonging

Poetry of Diaspora
in Silicon Valley
Volume 4

Disclaimer: This anthology is a compilation of poetry and artwork of diverse individuals. This book does not intend to disrespect any community, caste, religion, creed, nationality, or gender. Copyrights of each contributor's artwork, written words, and poetry remains perpetually with individual contributors while the book as a whole remains copyrighted by the press of which no part, other than attributed excerpts in book reviews, may be used or copied without explicit written permission.

COPYRIGHT © 2024 • ALL RIGHTS RESERVED
PIERIAN SPRINGS PRESS

Other than review quotes or academic excerpts,
no part of this work may be reproduced
without explicit permission.

FIRST EDITION, October 2024
ISBN 978-1-953136-92-3 PAPERBACK

Editor: Dr. Jyoti Bachani
Cover Graphic Design & Book Typography by Kurt Lovelace.
Cover artwork by PIERIAN SPRINGS PRESS.
Cover type *Bauhaus Dessau* **Alfarn** by Céline Hurka,
Elia Preuss, Flavia Zimbardi,
Hidetaka Yamasaki, and Luca Pellegrini.
Editor name in **Jenson** by Robert Slimbach.
Back Cover names in **Gill Sans Nova**.
Titles and body text set in **Baskerville**.
Flourishes set in Emigre Foundry **Dalliance** by Frank Heine.
Emigre Foundry **ZeitGuys** by Bob Aufuldish, Eric Donelan.
Typefaces licensed Adobe, Linotype, Emigre, & URW GmbH.

PSPRESS.PUB
PIERIAN SPRINGS PRESS, INC
30 N GOULD ST, STE 25398
SHERIDAN, WYOMING 82801-6317

Foreword

Being Becoming and Belonging is inspired by how the Poetry of Diaspora in Silicon Valley came into being as a vibrant literary group with interest in diverse languages and styles of poems. We existed for years before naming ourselves and using Facebook to coordinate our weekly meetings during the pandemic. Each of us was a passionate poetry lover but together we became something more - a committed, borderline addicted, bunch who gathered for hours to read and listen to poems being read aloud as a way to have meaningful dialog in verse about the most meaningful aspects of life and this world. Each of us is an independently creative artist, who also happened to find the company of other poetry lovers of this motley group irresistible and energizing. Many came and went but a core group emerged that became regulars, simply showing up as we were, sleepy, tired, excited, disturbed, elated, sad, happy, energized, just being ourselves, and craving the regular rhythms of our Saturday night ritual of poetic community. We belonged. None of us would have signed up for this had anyone planned this intentionally. We are too independent to wish to be a member of any Poetry Circle, yet we stepped up to host, agreed to read in public, co-created offerings for the community and encouraged each other. I decided to keep the lights on, the door open, to let all poetry lovers come and go as it suited them. When it lasted longer than I imagined possible. I decided to make the first volume as a family photo-album of poems. And here we are, with our fourth book, as if by some divine grace the book making too emerged to become an annual ritual.

Before Poetry of Diaspora in Silicon Valley existed, for almost a decade, I hosted poetry lovers in my living room, to read and converse in poems in different languages, some with translations. In 2020, when Covid sheltering-in-place orders were issued, instead of meeting in my home, as we were scheduled to, we just met in my online classroom. It became a weekly event instead of monthly, and every Saturday night for two years was spent with reading and listening to poems. It was difficult for me to coordinate weekly meetings so a Facebook group was created simply to ease our real shenanigans. At the end of the year I decided to make an anthology, just as a reminder of the memorable time we had spent together. As a pre-Google human, I felt that all that we had experienced in synchronous zoom sessions was somehow less real than meeting in person. It seemed to disappear into cyberspace like a poetic immersion dream. I needed a tangible object to hold in my hand to remind me that it was not just in ether and my imagination. The first anthology was the Memory Book of Poetry of Diaspora in Silicon Valley. It commemorated our time together with a paper sample of what might be read in one of our weekly meetings. I could hold it to know that the hours, weeks, months, years of poetry together actually happened. We are now meeting in-person again, about once a month.

The second anthology happened thanks to Kurt Lovelace and Praghalbha Doshi. By then Kurt had become one of our regulars and offered to publish our book through Pierian Press. Praghalbha volunteered to be the sutradhaar who organized the google folders and documents of all the submissions from the poets. She chose the title Starry Nights and it is her eyes on the cover of the book. Moitreyee Chowdhary clicked that picture on one of our evening walks at my favorite Shoreline Park. My role for that book was to connect each of our poetry stars who wished to be in the anthology to be there for it. The third book, called The Circle, was a gamble. I sent a call out for poems, not knowing if anyone would still be interested, as many had bloomed to be performing with other local groups or independently, with the confidence gained in this poetry incubator. I was surprised that enough poems were submitted to make The Circle. The cover had a painting by Moitreyee, which she had discarded a few years earlier. I liked its vibrant colors and large scale and had rescued it then. As I renovated my space, I offered it back to her, and she was grateful to reclaim her former artistic self. Such spontaneous collaborations and random actions of our everyday existence is how we sculpt each other and create the work we do. We just belong as the last of the creative and committed lot, who do this without any formal contracts, with no money changing hands, as a heart-centric ever changing collaboration, with enough sweat equity that we might legitimately claim to be crazy

Keeping company with so many creative folks and being exposed to so much poetry has changed me. I listen differently, nurture all creativity, and am a proud poetry mama who is happy to see 'my' poets in many public shows now, and a few of us have even been paid (token honorariums) to recite poems here and there. I am excited to be one of the featured poets at my alma mater Stanford University, for the South Asian Literature and Arts Festival 2024, in Encina Commons. I record this because my love for Hindi poems started in 1988 when a friend recited a Hindi poem for me in Encina Hall, but that is a story for another time. I accept this honor though translating poems is the fool's task I take on. My primary role has been as a community builder of this literary group and giving many poets the confidence they needed in early stages of their engagement with the world. I call them 'my' poets because many wrote and published their first articles about their love for poetry when I arm-twisted them into it. For a couple of years, I edited the Poetry as Sanctuary series for India Currents magazine and ensured as many of them got published as I could encourage.

We also spread our joy of poems by reading for the larger community around us. We have read poems at the Cupertino Diwali mela, at events hosted by Poet Laureates' of Cupertino and Belmont, by Mosaic America, Third Thursdays in Palo Alto, Chinese New Year Celebrations (to mark the friendship between Tagore and Xu Zimo) and our own home-grown series of online summer programs we co-created amongst us. The first one was designed by Sundeep Kohli with help from his talented family, and he called it Irshaad (2021). The next summer we re-interpreted it to offer Mukkarar (2022). By the third year, we had a sponsor, India Currents Foundation, as a partner with us over the shared agenda of "Stop the Hate". This program was called Navarasa (2023) for the nine emotions from classical Indian art treatise. This summer we offer the program for the well-being of all and called it Mangalam (2024). Poets from my circle have created their video series (Navaneet Galagali's Rasganga), poetry film (Sundeep Kohli's Hawai-Jahaaz), performed for San Jose Poetry Center sponsored Bauchaar series, for India Currents Foundation sponsored series, for the San Jose Art Festival, Mountain View Multicultural Festival and now the South Asian Literature and Art Festival, where four of us will be reading. I call this artistic group an incubator as many of our poets are causing ripples with poetry and other arts, writing, dance, painting, etc. in more ways than I can keep track of or claim credit for. I often wonder to myself how I got so lucky to have so many talented folks come to read in such amazingly curated poetry in my front lawn. I surrender to this magic with the attitude that perhaps by giving our breath to liberate poems from pages into the air, we get blessed by the poets before us. Afterall, Sindhis like me worship a 10th century poet as their chosen God, Jhulelal aka Sheikh Tahir or Lal Sai of the Dum-a-dum mast Qalandar dhamaal fame. The poems and the circle have a life of their own. I show up to do my thing and so do those who stay or leave my Circle. We have earned respect, been asked to make ourselves a logo, been paid to read poems to promote inclusion, and all things I never imagined doing.

While previous anthologies were simply a collection of submitted poems, this anthology was the first time when I sent a call for poems announcing a theme. We are ready to claim our identity as a collective that we have become. We have a culture that all poems are welcome, and deviating from themes is normal. This is how we show that we trust and cherish whatever emerges. It is enough to document the diversity of our voices at this specific time and place. We have the privilege to indulge ourselves in the rebellion of making poetry books. As the world had changed in so many ways after the Covid pandemic, I wondered if the others too had changed, like I have, from belonging to the poetry circle, or from life adjusting to the changed world around us. Here is what I wrote in the call for poems for this anthology:

"The kinds of poems that might make a thematic book can be about any of the following: You being you, as you are today, or as you were at an earlier time, recently or in the distant past. This need not be a personal poem as anything you care enough about to write a poem is your poetic self too - be it a tree, a language spoken by your ancestors, a poem about an ancient epic or poets you like, a famous bridge or a subject - like Chemistry, a status like being an immigrant, or emigrant, a parent, a child of refugee, being from a certain place, or time, be it the pandemic shift or an imagined place or this poetry circle.

If the first word in the theme, Being, is about what is stable in our world, then the second word, Becoming, is about all that shifts, and is changing. Poems of change, be it professionally, politically, economically, spiritually, physically or as embedded in any part of the world you consider yours or alien. We have experienced funerals, weddings, parenting, going back to school, starting new vocations, becoming home-owners, relocating across town or borders, travels abroad or back-home, becoming a first time parent or empty-nesters, taking a sabbatical, and many other life-changes and the experience of that is perfectly legitimate to document.

The third element in the theme, Belonging, is to bring in the rasas that make poems precious to everyone. Poems of loss and discovery, grief and joy, shame and glory, paradoxes and humor, beauty and disgust, trust and betrayals, confidence and fear, hot and cold, song and prose and belonging or not. The state of the world, the solutions to the wicked problems, the dreams, the imagined and the real."

In the following pages, the readers will find poets from places other than the Silicon Valley, as online word of mouth has engaged folks from other parts of the USA, from India and the United Kingdom. The poems are in many languages, Hindi, Urdu, (Hindustani) English, Marathi, Sanskrit, Latin/Spanish and some more. We have highly trained poets alongside those who have never taken a poetry class but may have a PhD in international business or math or no formal college training. The words are offered straight from the heart, because most of us have declared that the words choose us and come to us when they wish to. Even a casual reader will find sufficient variety in this anthology to like a line or a few. My biased opinion is that the discerning reader will find many gems. Dear reader, my wish is that you read knowing that no one fits into any box and yet we are not total strays either, because we know how to belong to poems. We indulge, enable and support each other enough to have co-created this, and more before this. I sincerely hope that you will find something you like or enjoy exploring the variety. All errors are mine. The non-existent buck stops here, with me. I have undertaken this labor of love to keep alive the practice of certain values, to nurture, co-create, commit time, energy, and whatever resources available. My expectation of the poets and poetry lovers holding this book is to be forgiven for its shortcomings. Thank you for being, becoming and belonging to poems.

Dr. Jyoti Bachani
California, September 2024

CONTENTS

Salma Arastu

वक्त का सैलाब 3
कुछ तुम कहो कुछ हम 4
धुप के टुकड़े 6
अमा 7
चाँद का रथ 8
रात ढल ही जाएगी 9
सूनी रात 10
प्रकृति का नियम 11
तपस्या 12
दीन 13
अभी नहीं 14
उत्पीड़न की कहानियां 15
मांओं की सेना 16
बाती 18

Kalpana Asok

We Did Not Have Cell Phones Then 21
The Shiny Ant–At Home In Yosemite 23

Jyoti Bachani

Poetry 27
Language Legacy For My Child 29
Angry For Love 30
Basant by Rohit Rusia 34
Untitled Poem by Rohit Rusia 36
Sambhavnayen by Atma Ranjan 38
Taki mere bheetar... by Nityanand Gayen 40
Chandini ki panch partain by Sarveshwar Dayal Saxena 42
Nidarr Aurten by Shuba Shuba 44
Chhipkali by Hussain Haidry 46

Moitreyee Chowdhury

- I belong to the scar ... 51
- In the Museum ... 53

Mona Dash

- Implications ... 57
- The Poet In Business ... 58
- Migrant Dilemma ... 59
- Not Knowing, Migration ... 60
- Turmeric ... 62
- Unbound Feet ... 63
- The Making of A Goddess ... 64
- For Plath, For Love ... 66
- Shakti ... 67
- A Certain Way ... 68
- Belonging ... 70
- Nostalgic Rain ... 71
- The Skin of Tradition ... 72
- Suitcases ... 74
- Διασπορά | Diaspora ... 76
- The Immigrant's Song ... 77
- Creator ... 78
- Shiva ... 79
- Durga ... 80

Pragalbha Doshi

- The Call to Shine ... 85
- The Silent Warrior ... 86
- Do I have a personality? ... 88
- Does it really matter? ... 90
- Envy & What can Be ... 91
- I can Be This & You can Be That ... 92
- Difference ... 93
- The trail behind me ... 94
- A Lazy Afternoon ... 95

Are Emotional Beings Fools? ... 96
Do Nothing ... 98

Gerardo Flores
Catullus: 101 ... 101

Anuradha Gajaraj-Lopez
Devotion ... 105
Gratitude ... 106
Sanyasi ... 107
She Stood By Me ... 108

Navaneet Galagali
Matrpanchakam ... 113
Krishnakarnamrtam ... 114
Bhagavad Gita ... 116
Hanuman Jayanti ... 117
Ganga Lahari ... 118

Reena Kapoor
She's Gone ... 121
Instructions For When You're Lost ... 122
Betrayals Of The Sun ... 123
The Postman ... 124
Speed ... 127
Smell, Like A Rake For Memories ... 128
Damn, Girl! ... 130
Words Like Oxygen ... 131
Love's Music In 100 Words ... 133
The Past Is A Country I Used To Know ... 134
Another Self-Improvement Quest? ... 136
Heart's Hometown ... 138
The Whole Universe Came Visiting ... 140

Monica Korde

Reasons for Using the Mango ... 145
Where the Flowers Fall ... 146

Smita Shekhar Korde

प्रेम म्हणजे ? ... 151

Vaishali Kulkarni

१. ... 155
जीवनाचा रंगमंच ... 156
बदल... ... 157

Lalit Kumar

Belongings ... 161
The Second Mountain ... 162
At the Crossroads ... 164

Kurt Lovelace

Παρουσία | Visitation ... 166
Traversé | Crossed ... 168
Au Cas où vous Obtiendriez cette Note à Temps ... 170
Fabulae | Fable ... 172
İstanbul'da Yön Bulmaya Çalışmak ... 174
お行儀 | Etiquette ... 175

Yogesh Patel

Gestalt Intelligence ... 179
Oracle ... 180
Cataracts ... 181

Kamala Tyagarajan
- Drive 185
- Roots and Wings 186
- Bond Energy 187
- By the Lakeside 188

Topaz
- Sic Ergo Sum 191
- 3rd Sutta of Siddhartha 192
- Sum Ergo Sic 193

Vishal Vatnani
- The River Walk 197
- It Doesn't Add Up 198
- A Snowflake Dining In Texas 199

Belonging

Salma Arastu

As an internationally exhibited woman artist, she brings a unique global perspective, having been born into the Sindhi and Hindu traditions in Rajasthan, India, and later embracing Islam and moving to the United States in 1986. As a woman, artist, and mother, she works to create harmony by expressing the universality of humanity through paintings, sculpture, calligraphy, and poetry. Her works are greatly influenced by her studies and experiences in different cultures around the world. After graduating in Fine Arts from **Maharaja Sayajirao University** in Baroda, India, she lived and worked in Iran and Kuwait, where she was exposed to a wealth of Islamic arts and Arabic calligraphy. Calligraphy, miniatures, and the folk art of Islam and the Hindu tradition continue to influence her work today.

As a visual artist, she has exhibited her work in over forty-five solo shows nationally and internationally, and won several prestigious awards including the **East Bay Community's Fund for Artists** in 2012 and 2014 and 2020. The City of Berkeley's **Individual Artist Grant Award** in 2014, 2015, and 2016. She has public art pieces on display in Bethlehem, Pennsylvania and San Diego, California. As an author, she has written and published five books of poetry. Her most recent work, on ecological consciousness from Quranic verses, is OUR EARTH: EMBRACING ALL COMMUNITIES.

वक़्त का सैलाब

कुछ पल ऐसे हैं मेरी यादों के शेल्फ पर
जो मुस्कान बिखेरते हैं मेरे लबों पर
और कुछ आँसू ढलका देते हैं आँखों से
कुछ पल दहशत के, उदासी के
तो कुछ पल मुझे बिना परों के उड़ा ले आते हैं गगन में
कुछ स्नेह के आँचल से बँधे
तो कुछ तेरी जफ़ा की दुहाई देते हैं
यादों के कच्चे धागों से बँधे
वक़्त के सैलाब से अक्सर उभर, उभर आते हैं
मेरी रफ्तार को सुस्त कर देते हैं
मेरा ध्यान बटा कर,
मैं उलझ, उलझ जाती हूँ बार, बार
जी तो कहता है कि सारे पलों को खींच कर
तोड़ कर कच्चे धागों को
हाथों से नैया बना कर बहा दूँ इस सागर में
फिर मन कहता है कि सीदूँ पूरे पलो को जोड़ कर
बना दूँ एक पैरहन
और ओढ़ लूँ जब, जब जी चाहे
कम से कम ये हर वक़्त की उलझन तो ख़त्म हो जाये

कुछ तुम कहो कुछ हम

किसी से एक बार मिलने से उसकी कहानी नहीं बनती
कुछ तुम वक़्त निकालो और कुछ हम
चँद मुलाकातें करें तो कहानी के सूत्र शायद जुड़ पायेंगे
कहानी जान पायेंगे, एक दूजे से जुड़ जायेंगे
कुछ तुम समझने की कोशिश करो और कुछ हम

इतनी जल्दी दरवाज़े बंद न करो
सांकल न चढ़ाओ, ताले न लगाओ
कहीं ज़ंग न लग जाये बरसो में
और दूर हो जाएं हम सदा के लिए
जुदा, जुदा तो जी ना पायेंगे हम
आओ कुछ तुम आगे बढ़ो तो कुछ हम

ये सच है कि
हम समझ ना पाये हैं एक दूजे को
हमारी सोच रँग दी गई है हमारी सदियों से चली परम्पराओं से
रुढ़िवादियों से, संस्कृतियों से
सहज नहीं है इन ऊँची दीवारों को तोड़ना
सदियों से जमी गर्द को धोना
पर कुछ तुम कोशिश करो और कुछ हम

गहराई से फैला धुंधलापन हमें एक दूसरे को देखने भी तो नहीं देता
और जन्मदाता का दिल भी तो है दुखता
एक ही घर से आये हैं हम
एक ही पिता की औलाद हैं हम
मिल जुल के रहें और समझें एक दूजे को
फिर कुछ तुम कोशिश करो और कुछ हम

जिस तरह बाँटते हैं हम हमारे माँ बाप की सम्पति
लड़ते हैं उलझ जाते हैं बराबर के बटवारे के लिए
फिर दाता की दी निआमतों को क्यों हड़पना चाहते हो तुम
अगर मैं आवाज़ उठाती हूँ तो क्यों गोली चलाते हो तुम
इस तरह कैसे जी पाएंगे हम
आओ कुछ तुम कोशिश करो और कुछ हम

धुप के टुकड़े

शिकायत खुद से नहीं
ज़माने से भी नहीं
तुझ से भी नहीं है मुझ को
शिकायत है तो बस इस घड़ी से है
बेरहम चलती ही जाती है
न रुक कर कभी मेरे जज़्बात को महसूसा
न मेरी तन्हाई को समझा
कई बार उसे उठा कर फेंका भी है
पर फिर देखा सूरज का डूबना उभारना जारी है
दिन पे रात
रात पे दिन सवार चलते ही जाते हैं
मैंने खिड़कियां, दरवाज़े भी बंद कर के देखे हैं
क्योंकि मुझे
सरकते वक़्त का एहसास भी न चाहिए
पर मैंने देखा
रोशनदान से धूप के टुकड़े लटकते आते हैं
क्या करूँ परेशान हूँ मैं
ये सच है कि शिकायत खुद से नहीं, ज़माने से नहीं
तुझ से भी नहीं बस इन धूप के टुकड़ों से है
जो मेरे पास जमा होते जा रहे हैं बेहिसाब

अमा

जो तूने दिया वो किसी ने न दिया
वो सिर्फ प्यार नहीं कुछ और भी है
वो सिर्फ ममता नहीं कुछ और भी है
वो सिर्फ कर्तव्य नहीं कुछ और भी है
वो सिर्फ तुम्हारी देखभाल नहीं कुछ और भी है
वो है विश्वास अपने आप में जो तूने दिया
हर मां दे सकती है अपनी संतान को पता नहीं
ये विश्वास कि तुम हो हकीकत और है ये संसार
जूझो डूबो उभरो अपने आप ही
सत्य की ताक़त लेकर
जगमगायेगा सूरज तुम्हारी आस लेकर
ये विश्वास ये साहस
तूने दिया और जो तूने दिया वो किसी ने न दिया

चाँद का रथ

वक़्त की धारा के साथ बहते हुए
कभी रुक कर मैं सोचती हूँ
कि मेरा बीता कल कहाँ है अब?
शाम की लालिमा जब आकाश पर छा जाती है
या चाँद का रथ जब खिड़की से गुज़रता है तो पल भर के लिए मैं खो जाती हूँ
मेरे गाँव के आँगन में भी इसी तरह
आकाश पर लालिमा और फिर चाँद का रथ गुज़रता होगा
रंगीन वो लिबास पहने बंजारिन
आँखों में चमक और होंठों पे गीत लिए
सुबह से शाम करती होगी
वो धूल उड़ाता कारवाँ
वो ऊँटों की क़तारें
 लहराते वो आँचल
बाबा कहते अच्छा बेटा,
अभी आते हैं हम
और बचपन का दिल उदास!
छत पर खड़े पतंगों की कतार को तकती वो आँखें
गोबर के उपले थोपती रही देहातिन
बच्चों के समूह कबड्डी खेलते
नल के पास घड़े लिए वो पनिहारिनें
वो झड़प, वो अनबन
वो लपककर फिर मिलन
प्यारे से वो दिन कहानियों की रातें
सब गुज़र गए हैं बीते कल के साथ
और आज जीवन की सुख सुविधा के बीच
भागती गाड़ियों और उड़ते वक़्त के बीच
जब कभी शाम की लालिमा और चाँद के रथ को तकती हूँ मैं
तो पल भर के लिए रुककर सोचती हूँ
कि मेरा बीता कल कहाँ है अब?

रात ढल ही जाएगी

सो जाओ, न ताको आसमानों को
रात की बेरहम गाथा न दोहराओ
हज़ारों गुनाह आँसू और तनहाइयों को
समेटे आँचल में
रात ढल ही जाएगी
अब तुम सो जाओ

सूनी रात

चाँद उभरने की बात उसने कुछ यूँ कही
कि चाँद डूबने की बात मैं उससे कह न सकी
रात तो सबके हिस्से में आती है बराबर
किसी की बिना चाँद की रात
तो किसी की चाँद की रात
किसी की रात लंबी होती है
तो किसी की छोटी से रात
ये हिसाब किताब हम तुम ही क्यों करते हैं?
रात तो उजाले की दीवानी
चली आती हर दिन के पीछे
और दिन फिर सरक जाता है
उसके करीब आने से पहले
रात तो सूनी है तनहा है
तुझ जैसी और मुझ जैसी
वो भी है ग़म खायी हुई
दोष उसे न दो

प्रकृति का नियम

आज सुबह मैंने देखा कि आसमां के दोनों ओर
रंग हैं अलग, अलग
एक तरफ लाली है तो दूजी और गेरुआ
शहर है बादलों के घेरे में
और पुल चमक रहा है उजली किरणों में
मानो प्रकृति फिर दे रही है संदेश ये समझा कर
कि मुमकिन है दो पहलू रहें हर वक़्त
बुराई और भलाई भी रहते हैं एक संग
हर नया पल है तुलना का पैमाना
तुम्हारे निर्णय से ही पहचाना जायेगा तुम्हारा रंग
कितना भी पलड़ा भारी हो बुराई का
डटे रहो न्याय और सच्चाई की राह पर

तपस्या

आशा की किरण डूबने न दो
 उम्मीद की लौ बुझने न दो
लाखों तूफ़ान आने दो
अपने अन्दर की आस को टूटने न दो
लहरें आज खामोश हैं तो क्या
 किनारों का बदन आज बेपर्दा है तो क्या
कल फिर मौजें उभरेंगी
संगीत लहराएगा फ़िज़ाओं में
उमडती लहरें आएँगी दौडते हुए
और ढँक लेंगी किनारे का बदन
आपने आँचल से
और खेलेंगी मन बहलाएंगी
तुम्हारा भी
आज की ख़ामोशी है तपस्या करने के लिए
उस ख़ालिक़ का शुक्र करने के लिए
 जिसे ज़िंदगी की लहरों के शोर में तुम अक्सर भूल जाते हो
आशा की किरण डूबने न दो
 उम्मीद की लौ बुझने न दो
लाखों तूफ़ान आने दो
अपने अन्दर की आस को टूटने न दो

दीन

हमने अल्लाह की वुसत और रहमत को इतना छोटा नाम क्यों दे दिया है?
कुछ ने कहा धर्म तो किसी ने कहा religion
सब अपनी, अपनी परिभाषा देते हैं इस नाम की
और बहस करते रहते हैं उसके वजूद की
उसके नाम के वजूद में तो समाये हैं सातों लोक और आसमान
यह धरती, यह सागर और भी कई अनजाने करोड़ों जहान
वो कैसे सिमट पायेगा तुम्हारे इन छोटे, छोटे शब्दों में
ये तो सिर्फ सिखाते हैं सलीके जीने के
जो उसने बताये हैं सदियों से सब को अलग, अलग
निहित है इन सलीकों में उस अछूते कारीगर का मक़सद
वो नहीं समाता इन परिभाषाओं में
सब परिभाषाएँ ख़त्म होती हैं उसकी वुसत में

अभी नहीं

थिरकती लहरें कहती जा रही हैं
एक पल झांको अपने अंदर भी
मस्ती भरी हुई है तेरे अंदर भी
आसमान अठखेलियां करते हुए बादलों के संग
झुक कर कह रहा है कि मेरी परछाई देखो
कभी आपने भीतर भी
हवाएँ भी हर सुबह गुनगुनाते हुए कहते जातीं हैं
संगीत की स्वर लहरिया जगाओ अपने अंदर भी
पर लम्बे, लम्बे पाँवों वाले वक़्त के साथ भागते, भागते
फूलती हुई साँस के साथ
बस मैं दोहराती रहती हूँ अभी नहीं
अभी नहीं
वक़्त आगे बढ़ जायेगा
अभी नहीं
अभी नहीं

उत्पीड़न की कहानियां

हत्या और गैर प्राण दंड की गाथाएँ
दुहराई जा रहीं हैं आज भी
हम मानव नहीं अगर हमारी आँख न भर आए
देख कर अत्याचार चहुँ ओर!
एक तरफ वैश्विक महामारी ख़तम कर रही है
 गरीब और लाचार एक जाति को
तो दूसरी ओर प्रशासनिक व्यवस्था
मार रही है उन्हें गला दबोच कर
क्या अफ्रीकन अमेरिकन जाति है धिक्कारने के लिए ?
लाये तो हम ही थे उन्हें उनके घर से खींच कर
लोहे की श्रृंखलाओं से बांध कर
गुलामी की बेड़ियों में जकड़ कर
क्या हो गया है तुम्हे ए मानवता ?
अब जागो
अपने जुर्म को क़बूलो
और ख़त्म करो ये गुलामी
जो तुम ने कागज़ पर तो मिटा राखी है
लेकिन छुपा के रखी है गहराई तक अपने अंतर में
अब जागो ए मानवता
ख़तम करो ये गुलामी

मांओं की सेना

खबरें सुनने को मन नहीं करता, इसलिए मैंने रेडियो और
 टेलिविज़न को बंद करके रखा था
पर खबरें, हिंसा की खबरें तो बेरोक टोक दोहराई जाती हैं
हर पल हर किसी के मुंह से...
किसी ने कहा सुना तुमने? आज बीस मासूम बच्चे गोलियों की
 अंधाधुंध बारिश में मारे गए हैं
दूसरी तरफ से आवाज़ आई सुना तुमने—एक अल्हड़
 लड़की छ भेढ़यो का शिकार बनी
दिल्ली की सड़कों पर एक बस में चलते चलते...
दंग हूँ मैं- परेशान हूँ मैं
रेडियो और टेलिविज़न तो मैंने बंद करके रखा था
पर इन गूंजती आवाजों को कैसे रोकूँ मैं?
कहाँ छुप जाऊँ मैं?
या फिर कान बंद कर लूं मैं?
पर नहीं मेरे कान बंद करने से या छुपने से
ये घृणास्पद कार्य तो बंद नहीं होंगे
और ना ही टेलिविज़न और रेडियो बंद करने से...
तुम माँ हो!
अंदर से एक आवाज़ आई की तुम माँ हो...
निर्भय ज्योति की टिमटिमाती आस को तुम कैसे तोड़ सकती हो?
उन बीस बच्चों की निगाहों में भरे भय को कैसे मिटा सकती हो?
वीर मलाला जो गोलियां खाकर भी ज्ञान पाने की तलब रखती है—
उसका साथ देने से कैसे पीछे हट सकती हो?
तुम माँ हो!
अंदर से एक आवाज़ आई की तुम माँ हो...
हिंसा को मिटाने के लिए तुम्हें सामने आना होगा
मर्द के क्रोध और वासना से पीड़ित हर नारी को जगाना होगा
कभी रौद्र रूप काली बन कर
तो कभी बीबी फातिमा का संयम ओढ़कर...

हर नारी को सचेत करना होगा आवाज़ दे देकर
ज्योति सिसक सिसक के कह रही है
माँ मेरे बदन को धो दो, मुझे पाक कर दो
यह आवाज़ गूँज रही है मेरे कानों में रात दिन
उठो मेरी बहनों इन भेड़यों को ख़ाक कर दो
मासूम बच्चों की हर आह पूछ रही है मानो-
इन राक्षसों को खत्म करने कब आएंगे सुपरमैन
नहीं बच्चों अब किसी सुपरमैन का इंतज़ार न करेंगे हम
मांओ की सेना लेकर मलाला के साथ ही जूझ परेंगे हम...

बाती

शमा जल उठी
एक बार फिर अंधेरे बुझ गये
कांपती लौ कर गयी ये शिकवा
रात ढलते ढलते
मेरा बदन जला कर तुम
कितनी रात और जियोगे
तेल खत्म हो रहा है बाती में

Kalpana Asok

Kalpana Asok, who lives and works in Silicon Valley, is a psychotherapist, author and poet. Her published works include WHOSE BABY IS IT, ANYWAY? INSIDE THE INDIAN HEART, which is a clinician's overview of the cultural and psychological functioning of South Asian diaspora families, and EVERYDAY FLOWERS, a chapbook of poems.

We Did Not Have Cell Phones Then

That bridge, you know, in Canada, Toronto maybe?
Across border.
We stood there, papa and me, in warm warm coats
With gloves and hats, red, so you could see at-once
That it is us, do you remember?

No? Yes? Ok. That day, we looked down, maybe I did
Don't know where papa looked, maybe at the sky
Blinking, blinking hard. And smoking.
I looked down waist level, looking for you
Then in white and blue with red scarf, I see you, but tall so tall
My height maybe more, not at belt level anymore.

We stood. We waved. You waved. We waved again.
I had stones in my mouth, my throat, my stomach.

> Darius,
> Do not shout at your mother. Rude, ingrate, how dare you.
> Do not do that. No more. Never. Sons don't shout at moms.

Let me tell you how it was

No phones no video phone. Just by-hand letters.
Uncle aunt fed me. Let me tell you. Not like moms.
No, not like moms.
Just like that 4 years, 6 years went.

Papa out of prison. The shah just gone. They let papa out.

So, they took me to see my parents from the edge of the border.
At the bridge, they came to see me. So, we could see across the fence.
At each other. Just stood. I yawned a lot they told me.
How long to stand there. 2 red blurs.
They gave me binoculars to see.
I needed glasses they told me.

I could not see so well.

She told me of the stones in her mouth.
I never shouted at her. Ever.

The Shiny Ant–At Home In Yosemite

The shiny ant walks to all four edges
of the warm rock

In shadow of the rock
moss clings to its north face
(Did you know you can find North
from the mossy sides of trees?)

In the shadow of the rock
Cushions of layered leaves spongy
as seaweed are tethered
by a minute pine root,
Holding on amid the pine needles

The desperately tiny seedling pushes
flowers and seeds for next year
hopeful before the summer heat
One of the millions of pine seedlings
just two needles strong now
Will she grow to make pinecones wastefully?

The delicate dogwood flowers catch
the sun letting you believe
just for a moment
that they exist
solely for beauty

The river rushes under the bridge as if it
    were made for rushing under bridges

The shiny ant has a meal in its pincers as it
    hurries off the cooling rock.

Jyoti Bachani

Dr. Jyoti Bachani is the founder of **Poetry of Diaspora in Silicon Valley**, a group of poetry lovers who meet regularly to read poems to each other. She is a strategy professor who professes that arts can humanize organizing. She has edited four poetry anthologies, guest edited the **Poetry for Organizing** special issue of the **Journal of Organizational Aesthetics** and translated over 200 poems from Hindi to English. She enjoys reading the poems by Vinod Kumar Shukla, Kunwar Narain, Sarveshwar Dayal Saxena, Ogden Nash, Hugh Prather, and many others. She enjoys listening to poems read out loud by passionate readers, in all languages.

Poetry

Poetry is for times
When words make no sense

Meaningful life must then be
Recreated by stringing
Absurdities in a rhyme
That keeps the memory
Of losses of our former selves

The rhythms from nonsense
Reconnect us to our heartbeats
To hear our laments, in silence
With attention undivided with anyone

Seeking the shards of words
That lost their meaning
In halted cadence of spaces on paper
Too dangerous to pick up the pieces of

In measured meters, gathering
Up the shattered dreams
That survive only in our imagination

Finding courage in the structure
Of a sonnet or a haiku
Looking for harmony in the
Maqktha *(final stanza)* of a ghazal
A note of peace in a geet *(song)*

Searching for understanding
To belong again by playfully embracing
What to hide even as we seek again
In the puzzles of connections

The songs that emerge from
The depths of our souls
Asserting that its okay to
Complain with our tongue

Sing of martyrs and revolutions
Keep our own promises
To never forget the pre-mature
Blows of the sculptor
Busy revealing the beauty within
In ugly times of violence

Poems to be committed to memory
To dance away the anger and spin into
Coerced forgiveness to let the sound
Churns out the multiverses
we respect from the Big Bang
That we choose afresh from.

Language Legacy For My Child

Finding no space for breath—in English
Only a faded memory of Hindi
With the taste of alien Punjabi
Saccharine and bittersweet
Hot-cold of distant extinguished Sindhi
They join their gypsy nomad tribe
In a quest for peace amongst the
Cities of artful beauty, with
Ancestors buried in pyramid lined avenues
Silently turning to the music within—Polyrhythms

Reaching for building a bridge between
The remnants of English that claimed one parent
And brought the other to youthful hungry Chinese
Leaving a blind teacher—Kavinoky to provide the shelter
Of freshly fluent Spanish—powered by the State
Under the watchful eye of a racist criminal.
Can languages matter to us: the silenced?

Angry For Love

Sins I can't forgive
grudges I carry within
keep my heart supple

Knowing it beats for some

Anger that fuels action

Inaction that prevents me
From spewing venom

To be reminded by a poem
"Lord, you granted me a tongue
May I never use it to complain."

Building dreams with my words
To show our healing
Resides in our hands

We survive, we thrive, we sing
The saddest most poignant songs

We write of the absences
To share with whoever has
Patient hearts to listen
With their embodied presence

The vacuums that we fill
With the never ending longings
Of tears we can never shed

The love that was stolen
From innocent children

Helplessly blissful at the
Mere presence of air within
Their lungs, power of eyes
To observe the random
Acts of kindness of strangers
Who understood the wrongs
That we were unaware of

Or denied to ourselves

To exist for long enough
Even with self-sabotage

That would take a lifetime
To acknowledge and maybe
Another to undo, to fill the
Black holes that we attract
As part of our radiance

With names we were given to
Cover up the destruction
Nikunj the sun
Jyoti the light
Ladoo Gopal the lord of innocence
Vishnu the preserver of life

Learning to take pride in
Speaking alien tongues
To avenge the humiliations
Heaped on our creators
By ambition for material aspirations
For validation, by branded goods with
Stories of manipulation
By the world that profits
From destruction,
In the name of development

Rebuilding, rewiring rehabilitation
Sell as drugs concerts fancy vacations
We don't get any satisfaction from
Even as we effortlessly accomplish
The fish bowl goals in our ever expanding
Endless quest beyond where men have gone before

In the darkness that prevails in this Universe.

Basant

Jab mile
Hum dono
Kisi ne
Kuch bhi nahin kaha

Tum aayeen
Bahney laga jharna
Tum muskarayeen
Khil gaye
Saare phool

Main chup chaap
Mahsoos karta raha
Basant
Apne bheetar

Hindustani Poet: Rohit Rusia

Spring

When we
Met
No one
Said anything

You came
The brook bubbled
You smiled
The flowers
Bloomed

I, silently
Experienced
The spring
Within

Translation: Dr. Jyoti Bachani

Untitled Poem

Paavon ke
Guzarney se
Pagdandiyan
Majboot ho jaati hain
Pani ke
Guzarney se aksar
Pukkey raastey toot jaatey hain

Hindustani Poet: Rohit Rusia

Untitled Poem

With feet
Passing
The trail
Becomes
A firmer
Path.

With water
Passing
Often
Paved roads
Are washed
Away.

Translation: Dr. Jyoti Bachani

Sambhavnayen

Dekhi he jaani chaahiyen
Humare aas paas
Har sambhav
Dekhi jayengi
Tabhi bach payengi

Sambhavnayen

Jaise andey ke bheetar rahti hai
Aakash vyaapi udaan
Jaise beej ke bheetar rahta hai
Chantar vat vriksha

Dekhi jayengi
Tabhi bach payengi

Hindustani Poet: Atma Ranjan

Prospects

Have to be seen
Around us
At every possible chance

For to see it
Is to save it

Prospects

Like the egg contains within it
The prospect of the sky-high flight
Like the seed contains within it
The prospect of a banyan tree

Only by seeing it
Can possibilities be preserved

Translation: Dr. Jyoti Bachani

Taki mere bheetar baccha rahe kewal sach

Aao tum
Meri talaashi le lo
Kahan chupa rakha hai
Maine jhoot ko
Use khoj lo
Mujhe sazza do
Taki mere bheetar baccha rahe
Kewal sach

Taki tum phir kabhie na
kah pao
Mujhe jhoota!

Hindustani Poet: Nityanand Gayen

So Within Me Only The Truth Remains

You are invited
To search me
For where I have hidden
Untruths
Find them
Punish me
So within me
Only remains
Just the Truth.
So you can never again
Call Me
A liar.

Translation: Dr. Jyoti Bachani

Chandini ki panch partain

handani ki paanch paratain
Har parat agyaat hai

Ek jal main
Ek thal main
Ek neelaakash main
Ek aankhon mein tumhare jhilmilaati
Ek mere ban rahe vishwaas mein

Kya kahun
Kaise kahun
Kitni zara si baat hai

Chandani ki paanch paratain
Har parat agyaat hai

Ek jo main aaj hoon
Ek jo main ho na paaya
Ek jo hone nahi dogi mujhe tum
Ek jo main ho na paunga kabhi bhi
Ek jiski hai hamare beech ye abhishapt chaaya

Kyun sahun kab tak sahun
Kitna kathin aaghaat hai

Chandani ki paanch paratain
Har parat agyaat hai

Hindustani Poet: Sarveshwar Dayal Saxena

Moonlight Is Five Deep

Moonlight is five deep
Each layer unknowable!

One in water
One on earth
One in the blue sky above
One twinkling in your eyes
One in my growing trust

What shall I say?
How shall I say it?
It is such a subtle thing!

Moonlight is five deep
Each layer unknowable!

One as I am today
One as I could not become
One as I will never become
One as you will never let me become
One as this cursed shadow between us

Why should I bear it?
How long should I bear it?
It is such a master stroke!

Moonlight is five deep
Each layer unknowable!

Translation: Dr. Jyoti Bachani

Nidarr Aurten

Hum auraten chitaon ko aag nahin detin
Kabbron pe mitthi nahin detin
Hum auraten marre huon ko bhi
Bahut samay jeevit dekhti hain

Sach to yeh hai
Hum maut ko lagbhag jhoot maanti hain
Aur bichadne ka dukh
Hum khoob samajhti hain
Aur bichdey huon ko
Hum khoob yaad rakhtin hain
Ve lagbhag sa-shareer humari
duniyaon main chaltey phirtey hain

Hum janam deti hain
Aur isko koi itna bada kaam nahin maanti
Ki humari puja ki jaye

Zhaahir hai
Jeevan ko le kar hum kaafi vyast rahti hain
Aur humara rona-gana
Bus chalta he rahta hai

Hum na to moksh ki iccha kar paati hain
Na bairaagi ho paati hain
Hum narak ka dwaar kahi jaati hain

Saare rishi muni pundit gyaani
Sadhu aur sant narak se dartey hain

Aur hum narak main janam deti hain
Is tarah yeh jeevan chalta hai

Hindustani Poet: Shubha Shubha

Fearless Women

We women do not light the funeral pyre
Throw dirt on the graves
We women, those who are dead for a long time,
see them alive

The truth is that,
we consider death
Almost as a lie
And the pain of separation, we
Understand really well
And those who are separated, we
Remember a lot
Almost as corporeal presence
Walking amongst our worlds

We give birth and we consider It not a big deal
Making us worthy of being worshiped

Its obvious with life
We keep pretty busy
And our crying-singing
Just keeps on ringing

We cannot aspire for moksha
Nor become ascetics

We are labeled the gateway to hell
All sage-wisemen, learned pundits
Ascetics and saints fear hell

And we give birth in hell
This is how this life progresses.

Translation: Dr. Jyoti Bachani

Chhipkali

khaaki rang deewaaron
par latakti Gandhi ji
ki badi-si photo ke
peeche se dupahri mein
eik lambi bhoori-si
Chhipkali nikali hai

reng kar khamoshi se
ird-gird photo ke
gasht ye lagaati hai

aur jaise hi koi
keet-patanga udd kar
paas se guzarta hai
dhar-daboch leti hai
pankh noch leti hai
maans chaba jati hai
zinda nigal jati hai

phir bade saleeqe se
jaise kuch hua na ho
koi bhi maraa na ho
rengti hui vaapas
Gandhi ji ki photo ke
Peeche laut jaati hai

Hindustani Poet: Hussain Haidry

Chameleon

Khaaki colored wall
With a large photo
Of Gandhi ji[1]
From behind which
At midday a large
Brown Chamelon crawls out

Quietly, it surveys
Here and there
Near the photo
For any moth or mosquito
Flying by, to
Snap off its head
Peel off its wings
Devour its' flesh
Swallow it alive

Then smartly, as if
Nothing has happened
No one has died
It sneaks back
To return behind
Gandhi ji's picture

Translation: Dr. Jyoti Bachani

---

[1] ji is an honorific added to someone's name to show respect, somewhat similar to being called Sir in English.

Moitreyee Chowdhury

Moitreyee is a psychotherapist and artist. She is passionate about building a community, that recognizes the beauty of diversity and works towards equity. Moitreyee enjoys meeting friends from across the globe, learning new languages, art, poetry, and wandering amongst tall trees. She seeks to understand the amalgamation of science, literature, arts, nature, and its relationship with the world.

I belong to the scar

A poem to be written that talks about belonging.
I touched the scar on my forehead.
The staircase of my first home
Amongst the narrow lanes of Pahargunj.
There lived a family of many.
And I belonged to those many.
The scar on my forehead was born there.
A child, walking, jumping, down the dark staircase
    of 1924 Paharganj.
A small Accident. Pain forgotten.
She played there; amongst many.
The scar now belonged to her.
She belongs to the scar.
Playing, gathering scars.

The scar on the arm.
People coming together. An accident.
A rickshaw story. Life survived.
The scar remained to talk about strangers coming together,
The child belonged that day to all those on the street.
Their scars met mine. It went deep. Merging, forming.
There are scars on the belly. A life formed.
Living, dying and again, starting many times.
I belong to that scar, of unformed cries.

The scars of heart. Formed as they do. Time and again.
Over decades, over centuries.
Creating, working its magic.
I gather the stories, reading, writing, living,
holding the hand of my scars,
We belong together.

World in chaos.
Scarring earth and all those who belong to her.
Far away. Scars form in the heart of the crying child.
The helpless, desolate Ma, with scars in her heart.
How do I show, that their scars belong to me as well?
I belong to those scars too. Forming, deepening. Hurting.
I run my hand over those scars.
The unseen and the seen. Merging with mine. Remaining.

In the Museum

You put my ancestors in a museum
You looted my land,
gathered my ancestor's soul,
you decided to bring them to your other looted land,
my Ganesha,
my Parvati ma,
You put them in a museum.

The lighting is beautiful.
Decorated and well designed.
I bought tickets to see
my Ganesha,
my Parvati ma
living in the museum.

You never took shoes off.
I could not take my shoes off.
My Ganesha,
my Parvati ma,
my ancestors.

Light is beautiful.
I am here with you.
In the museum

Mona Dash

Mona Dash is an award-winning author of LET US LOOK ELSEWHERE, A ROLL OF THE DICE: A STORY OF LOSS, LOVE AND GENETICS, A CERTAIN WAY, UNTAMED HEART, and DAWN-DROPS. Mona has work published in international journals and more than thirty-five anthologies. She works in a global tech company and lives in London.

Visit her author's page at
www.monadash.net

Implications

Born and raised an Indian; not living in India
                implied: *not Indian*
now British, not born in Britain
                implied: *not British*
a mother, working full-time
                implied: *not a mother*
a sales manager, a mother
                implied: *not a sales manager*
a woman, a mother
                implied: *not a woman*
a poet, a businessperson
                implied: *not a poet*
an engineer, an artist
                implied: *not an engineer*
becoming more than I was meant to
                implied: *a sense of erosion*
Venn-diagram like I seek
                implied: *commonalities*
finding intersectionality
                implied: *a pinpoint*

The Poet In Business

The poem in me
As if a silk scarf
Over a winter coat
      Unnecessary
      Fragile
      Bound to slip away
While I stand, crisp shirt
Tucked away neatly
Hair razor-sharp edged
Not one fly -away
Sky high stilettoes
      Unsteady .
      Impractical
      Power
Painted long nails
A circle of a gold
chain, neat studs
As my voice drills numbers
Long excel sheets
Numbers, revenues,
Quarter on quarter
Success
Stockmarkets
Perfect the role
Perfect the actor
Perfect the businesswoman

And the poem
Learns to stay a whisper
Just in passing
Just a flash of rainbow
Gone too soon
But not forgotten

Migrant Dilemma

Which country will I worry for
Which country should I cry for
The one I left, always home
The one I came to, forever home
If turmoil happens on every shore
Which one should I think about more?
Mourning in the morning
Or night time worrying
All over the world
A single narrative winning

And where did you all go
You poets and painters and singers
You asked us to imagine
and you left us asunder

Not Knowing, Migration

The Banyan tree and the Oak
know the same language

Migration
is not an answer
nor a question
but a movement:
birds leave and return

Passport engraved with a stamp
coloured, dated. I
booked a ticket, landed in a country
closer to the poles from a country
closer to the equator

I didn't know
I would collect theories and words
presumptions and assumptions
on my back
like a feathery creature
feathers firm on the body
plucking one out
draws blood

Wonder why, how, I became
so many things at once
Emigrant, Immigrant, Migrant, Subaltern
theories/concepts to luxuriate, nest in
I didn't know
that I am invisible
when I enter a room I didn't know
 I could be invisible in a room

I didn't know
the philosophers, post-colonists
have labelled behaviour
branded my very soul
Hybridity, Provincialism, Orientalism
my shadows, my silhouettes defined
before I knew

Two-headed Janus
looking out, looking in
from where we came
to where we came

I didn't know
I thought i was I
I was i

I thought I defined my self
I thought I was just I

Turmeric

I see these days,
On shop shelves, flavours of peach and turmeric
in little Kefir shots
Cranberry seeds and turmeric,
 masques in recyclable pots

Turmeric tastes on the tongue, lingering in infinite swirls
like Jazz, Renaissance, the Beat. A turmeric rage grows
in homes, health shops, the patents, the recipes, lotions
on skin, turmeric in all its fine avatars

Somewhere, they love yellow milk, drink
    an aphrodisiac in a tall glass
team fish soft in thin gravy, liquid gold on shining white rice
and brides apply a creamy yellow paste wanting to look fair

I see these days
the turmeric rhetoric owned by many
I don't say how I remember
my mother's fingers, her tiny nails
bitten to the quick,
mixing fish heads, pumpkin flowers
with turmeric stains on the nail bed and folds

Yellow stains left on handles and plates and clothes
like on this scarf; her finger tips golden dots, from far-away home.

Unbound Feet

First they bound our feet
bones broken into bite sized bits
chicken-wing dust post-dinner
flesh putrefied, perfumed
placed in lavish silk shoes
so small so beautiful
butterfly feet
that cannot stand firm
that cannot run
battered warped
lily-feet

then they didn't bind our feet
they just made sure when we ran
we were laughed at
when we tried to stand firm
the ground was pulled away
craters and venom beneath
then boulders tied to feet
we were pushed into the soil
living burial
even as we stand

soon they didn't have to try hard
the cages they grew us in
the boxes they stifled us in
broke our bodies and our breath
so they didn't have to.

The Making of A Goddess

resplendent goddess
when you become
we will worship you
with flowers, the best
roses, we shall decree
lotuses, pink-gold, fifty-five petals no less
incense mesmerizing intoxicating
only the pure can visit
they must fast a whole day and half
pine, plan for a year or two
before they visit you

we will enshrine you in marble
from European shores
inlaid lapis lazuli, outside
peacocks in the garden
fountains bursting colours
we will worship you
your visage, your body anointed
in red, yellow
your face smooth turmeric paste
our lives, our desires, our dreams
shall writhe at your feet

we will worship you
in return you must burn
first from the inside:
dry out the desire
that keeps you awake
dried-twig-like crush under your feet

those dreams that glisten
forgotten in your eyes
thoughts that anger
want to tear you apart
you must wash it out
wring yourself bone-dry
the hard bones you must crush
until they cannot support
and you will crawl
jelly-like amorphous moulding
the way we want you to

next your skin
it must burn
flake, curl into itself
beautiful eyes unseeing
hands crippled
breast waist fingers lips
conjoined mass

you must burn
the insides the outsides
the brain the mind the soul
the heart the earlobes
the swirls of your stomach
the legs and the in between
consuming fire
burnt, suffering, left with nothing
nothing.

But now you are a goddess
we will worship you

For Plath, For Love

(Don't)
 Let us then recite Plath's poetry
Let us wear white bikinis and smile
up at the sky, blue in our hearts as in the heavens
Let us sing mad girl love songs and in its rhymes
search thunderbirds, hold the bird close
dip into its heart, tasting its blood, yours, mine
Let us find these Hughes like men who love
deeply, amorously, thick-honey words
that choke so well, filling us, filling us
with still, deep water, cleansing and drowning
who know how to twist deep into us, severing
every self-belief, every little hope we have
burning away the mind-body-soul chain

(Don't)
 Let us write, write crazily into the night
and let our words howl in the still dawn
and let us then open the oven door
and lie ourselves in, breathing in purist like
a single strain of air, lying still then, lying still
while our children are in their beds, dreaming
                              dreaming.

Shakti[2]

One day you will see
—the Neelakurinji flower that blooms blue, once in twelve years
—the Aurora Borealis that flashes across cold still skies
—the Mariana Trench's secret life in its blackest depths
—metal glowing gold in the fire, carbon pressed into diamond
—the pyramid of Mount Kailash and the peak of the Himalayas
You will see it in my eyes; the past, the future, both in this present
You will see it on my mouth, you will see it
    on my face, glowing forehead,
where the mountains and trees and sun and moon
    and stars are etched
and your very gaze will change.
You will see. Me. One day. In this life
                     or many lives after
                     In me. Shakti.

---

[2] power, energy, or force. Mythologically, Shakti is always described as feminine, often personified as the goddess, Devi, the divine feminine consort of the divine masculine god Shiva. But at the deepest level, Shakti transcends gender.

A Certain Way

As an immigrant,
I am expected to behave in a way
a certain way.

Colour the walls with turmeric,
fill my soul with lament
for the land whose shores I have left
to become richer economically
poorer emotionally.
Fold oil into long black hair,
dream the stars of the eastern skies,
in this land, the land I call my own,
but never to be my own.
Wrapped in sarees,[3] sapphire blue, *sindoor*[4] red,
meant to be nostalgic about the
monsoon spray dazzling my eyes
calming my burning skin.

 Instead, my mind
soothed by the nourishing cool green
of the land I live in,
energised by the glowing orange sun
of the land I come from,
decorates ice cubes with spice.

---

[3] garment of southern Asian women that consists of several yards of lightweight cloth draped so that one end forms a skirt and the other a head or shoulder covering

[4] red or orange-red powder that is used in Hindu religious and cultural practices, and is a symbol of marriage for Hindu women

With silver anklets, red stilettoes,
the shortest, blackest dress,
I sip prosecco, spear olives expertly,
pile plates with rice and chicken curry
while in the garden
lavender, jasmine, clematis, and marigold,
spread their roots, dance their petals
into the pale grey wet skies
and the searing sunshine.

Uproot, grow, take root
parallel truths, a little of this,
a little of that.
For an immigrant,
there is no certain way to be.

Belonging

Corporate men, pinstripe suits
in deep discussion, in accents
lilting French, baritone German, twangy American.
Among them an Indian, worse, a woman, Indian.

When I speak in tone, walk with the step
eyebrows raise, they lean forward to hear better,
talk louder when addressing me, as if I am deaf
telling me silently:
You shouldn't be here.

A crowded English pub, people
standing in spaces too small for them.
I order the drinks.
The bartender stares when I say
'A glass of red wine and three pints of lager'
looking confused, leaning forward closer
telling me silently:
You shouldn't be here.

Welcoming smiles, women in sarees,
grinding masalas, rolling chapatis,
television is the world, content
in the four walls, within set boundaries.
My hometown, my roots, so far from my branches.
Ill at ease I sit
listening to my own voice
telling me silently:
You shouldn't be here.

Nostalgic Rain

An almost tropical rain arrives,
I watch from the window.
Quiet roads, quieter cars.
The almost tropical rain
adorns the hanging planters.
Colourful flowers, petunias, azaleas, fuchsias
but fragrance less,
so the rain awakens nothing, hidden.
There's even a hint of hailstones in today's rain.

But, to be truly tropical you
need to emerge from the hunger of heat
the acridity of drought.
You need to rise deep from ponds brimming with lotuses
form clouds that spray down at will, lustily.
An almost tropical thunder today.

But to be truly tropical you
need to have been conceived in despair
spawned in hunger.

You need to have it in your belly.

The rain beats down today,
my silence
it is not the same.

The Skin of Tradition

1

The foreigner watches a wedding in fascination
large *bindi*[5] squatting on her forehead
red saree colouring white limbs.
The elders enthuse how she
sits relaxed on the dusty ground
reveres the sacredness of every chant
embraces chaos in wondrous happiness.

The Americans, Germans, English,
French, Italians flock here, hearts one
with conch shells; cross-legged,
slurp white rice and dal from banana leaves.
Yet I, I ask for my fork and spoon.
Yet I, born in a small town, tempered by heat,
coloured with tradition, married saree-clad
 in front of the fire, complain of the fumes
my eyes burning. I, brought up within these walls
makes it a point to question too much
why should I, why must I, bow in respect,
 hide in shame, follow rules and customs,
 forget myself. I question for years.

Later, in London, that city I call home,
forgetting, at home *tulsi* plants sit in courtyards
white *chita* is drawn on Thursday
 to welcome Lakshmi.[6]
'A city without temples scratching its skyline
cannot be home ever,' they pronounce.
I question for years.

---

[5] a decorative mark worn in the middle of the forehead by Indian women
[6] Hindu goddess of abundance; Lakṣmī, in Sanskrit: "she who leads to one's goal"

2

The answer, thought but not mouthed:
You can appreciate culture,
fold your legs in suppliance
bend your head, fast all day in a temple
knowing tomorrow you will be home.
Today is a thrill, like climbing Machu Picchu
like rowing down the Okavango delta.[7]
When the blood that runs in you today
bled on a pyre, hundreds of years ago
soaking chrysanthemum garlands
when a village is somewhere, had you lived
fifty years before, you would be
behind a veil waiting, watching,
when not that many years back, a marriage
marked you with blood red *sindoor* in black hair
closeted rooms, opened legs
breeding healthy sons and if not white widows.

When you know all this, then, the legs don't fold here
in the dust, in the sacredness
even though they do at Yoga in the gym.

The heart that belongs, never accepting, runs,
runs the farthest,
to shed centuries of old skin.

---

[7] a vast inland river delta in northern Botswana. It's known for its sprawling grassy plains, which flood seasonally, becoming a lush animal habitat.

Suitcases

battered suitcases
tightly packed, transoceanic
oversized chocolate tins, shortbread
spirits, perfumes duty free
lego, whittard teas
fortnum mason jams, l'occitane lotions
nestling in muslin gift bags

gifts rationed
familial smiles, knowing shrugs
for everything is here
zara, mango, earl grey, body shop
Chanel, yes everything
the world is here
the shelves are full

unspoken words
why did you leave
why did you love other lands
thoughts refracting
prisms, chants in minds
betrayal, traitor, traitor

smells, airs
living in another world
deciding between worlds
smoothly blend in? nourish identity?
gauged, studied, here, there
a single comment
opening Pandora boxes
of reactions

they go, they come
unknowing, large suitcases
migratory birds, looking for homes.

Διασπορά | Diaspora

The place we live in
has a name
no geography, no laws

        The contours touch
        several boundaries
        suspended over oceans

The inhabitants
straddle worlds, legs in one
minds in the other
souls here

        Emblems of countries
        in red, blue, and black
        disparate identities

In this drifting space
sometimes we tilt
we shift towards
where we came from
sometimes we sink
into new lands

        Floating, disjointed
        mass
        no names, no roots
        only a scattering
        seeds swept by a tuft of hair
        a dispersion

The Immigrant's Song

When it rains here,
in this country, with its dark earth,
rainbow gardens,
sometimes the flecks of rain
touch the earth just like in the dusty Indian plains.
Fresh waters soak into the hungry soil.

The smell! Like when clouds break and it's monsoon
in India, the heat of the plains dissolving in the waters.
The smell of long ago, the smell of home.

Suddenly, this country with its different skies
roses in the summer, lights in the winter,

becomes home, as well.

Creator

Your first born
was grotesque
Arms spanning the world
crushing it with iron strength.
Your second born
was fierce
exploding fire from his mouth
burning souls in a day.

The ones who came after
and after
raged for days
destroying the fabric of the skies
the foundations of forests
ripping sturdy mountains
until the streams dripped blood.

Still, you didn't stop.

You carried on
producing offspring

one after the other
advancing across geographies
changing histories
living unimagined futures.

Until one day, they swallowed the sun
whole, shredded the earth
and washed away the paintings
of your image
Until one day they brought apocalypse
in the middle of the *Yuga*.

Shiva

Creator, destroyer, passive, fierce,
contradictions live in you, mirroring
the world around,praying to you.
A giver of boons, of wishes
indiscriminately perhaps.

Your devotees surround your form
snakes coil on your neck.
We bow to the
ash smeared, unwashed ascetic
Lord of Dance.

You live here as well,in this country
even in this antiseptic calmness.

In these well-ordered gardens,
sometimes a glimpse of a tail
of the King slithering,an angrythunderstorm
music to your fierce dancing.

Sometimes the sun scorches,
sometimes floods ravage.
The Destroyer in you.

But it's comforting,
whether in anger or in calmness
to see Shiva in this land
to know the all-pervading
everything of Shiva here, as in that
distant Himalayan land.

Durga[8]

It was only for an instant
that she forgot to breathe.
At that moment
the seas sucked through and dried
leaving craters of drought.
Hearts collapsed, exploded
pralaya in our lives.
Perversions took human form
as men, demon-like

gouged and penetrated.
Women ruptured into
mangled, grieving parts.
Stones, blades, rusty hammers
lodged in fragile bodies.

Durga! Mother!
Singhabahini! [9]

She forgot to see
her eyes shut for a moment
and at that instant
the world was sucked into
the writhing abdomen of the
asuras.[10]

---

[8] Hindu goddess who is often depicted as a warrior goddess. Her name comes from Sanskrit and literally translates to "impassable, invincible, or unassailable"

[9] the Goddess Singhabahini, who is depicted as a metallic pitcher, worshiped by those seeking self-purification and eternal peace

[10] a member of a class of divine beings in the Vedic period, which in Indian mythology tend to be evil

Those lustrous eyes will open
benedictions shower
as we chant to Her.

Durga! Mother!

New worlds live.

Pragalbha Doshi

Pragalbha Doshi lives with her family in San Jose, CA, and works as a therapeutic yoga teacher (E–RYT500, yogasaar.com). Poetry came as an expression of awakening and healing to her. It brought alive to her the nature of existence and the world in relation to life. Inspirational and soothing are two common responses to her writings.

Her poetry appears in various anthologies, and Pragalbha is the co-editor of Poetry of Diaspora in Silicon Valley 2022 Anthology, named STARRY NIGHTS. She also contributes articles to **India Currents** and **American Kahani** magazines. She posts regularly on her blog **Infinite Living** at pragalbhadoshi.com.

The Call to Shine

It is amusing when we sometimes avoid someone
because they would make sense

It feels comfy to be in the Cute-but-not-so-bright
state of being, for a while more

Thank you to the twinkling stars that continue to beacon me
Yes all of you who continue to inspire me

I will be home I promise, I'll join you
Let me play a bit more, it's just fun to

I will find the courage to shine bright
And maybe become a beacon for few more

The Silent Warrior

I have it in me to win this game
I know very well patience is its name
Never quit never give up
I got this, this is my cup

This attitude keeps my spirits up
Gives me power gives me passion
Intoxicates me with strength and also its illusion
I will fight this because I got it down in my pride
I have got my will by my side

Equipped myself with all the defenses
Earned on the way all the praises

Gratitude and Kindness became my allies
Exchanging both with others made miracles arise

There's always this fear though that lingers
If I can sustain the anchors
At times really breaks me down
And the best that we have as Seekers

One more ally called Surrender
Would make it all very easier
What would it be like to let go
To be able to join the universal flow

Challenges me to do so
The 'I' is not easy to let go
Have to admit it sounds a relief
To have to do no more
To just be the Being at the core

Strength and passion not felt as a surge
Universe becomes the fuel
That with which you merge
Willpower gets to rest
Freedom at its best

Passion is more like this silent power
Strength like this inert confidence
Faith is more like this inner knowing
I am now at peace and also still the same warrior

Do I Have A Personality?

Do I have a personality?
I grew up feeling none.
I kept wanting one.

I saw some as persons happy
But I felt lot of thoughts unhappy
I saw some as being persons assured
But I felt unsure of what really mattered
I saw some as being persons positive
But I felt I needed lot more perspective
I saw some wearing their wealth on them
And I felt the need to become abundant
I saw some wearing their success on them
But I felt I really wish I had a passion
I sought to be truthfully joyful
But I felt lot of things to be untruthful

I simply only wanted my own personality
Yet I tried every which way to fit in
Also learned some tricks to blend in
Wherever I Be I became that one
Except it became difficult to keep up

Do I have a personality?
Now supposedly a grown-up
I am not sure I have one

A new friend in conversation
In complete awe of my hard-core choices
Called me in myself an institution
And visiting me a few days later
Found me a sobbing mess of confusion

Befuddled she said to me
"Never imagined You could become this"

I confided in her honestly
I needed the friend in her
As much as she used the one in me.
She probed further if I had ever cried
For those times such and such
I said yes I did
When at times I became human as much

This kind friend then exhorted me
That I should be wearing all that I am
And walk out in the world head held high
Gain some confidence and personality

Veracity in the moment doesn't allow me
To wear anything external on me
I am that I am and I wonder what I am
I live in an attempt of absolute integrity
In all the roles that can be called of me
I show up with confidence or confusion
It is me in that moment feeling fluidly
The only corrugation is of my intention

So now do I have a personality?
You tell me which one you see in me
So do I need a personality?
Or I could just Be what I have come to Be

Does It Really Matter?

When you feel like you want to disappear
What you really want is to arrive and appear
In a way that is totally you
You with all of yourself and facades few

You try to get away from it all
You though keep hearing a call
To show up this place and that
Coats and scarves and maybe a hat
You reach for things that cover best
Now that your presence is put to test
Yeah I know it is the season and weather
But how glad you seem to veil altogether

It is rather amusing to me
When I hide myself to deter
And then see how many check or bother
It shows my innate desire
To show up with all my fire
But just want to disappear
Because I am not sure if it does matter

Envy & What Can Be

All that you envy, it is very possible to achieve

All that you can Be, is impossible for others to perceive

Simple reason to keep Being what you truly can Be

And that is how you might become the one envied

But then you become oblivious to the very concept of Envy

I Can Be This & You Can Be That

If I can be this and here
Whatever and wherever you see me
You too can be that and there
Whatever and wherever you want to be

Just ask those who had met me
Before I simply started living and being me
You will know how small and low I lived
Before I let go of the fear of not fitting in

They will tell you how hard it is to believe
Who is this and what really happened
To the one who did not have a clue
To the one, either too dumb or too loud

I only wish to keep being this and here
Centered in this labyrinthine life of desire
Immersed in what feels like flawless space
Living as the energy that happens to have a face

Evidence that you can be this and that and there
Whatever and wherever you want to be…

Difference

I used to remain small
to keep others comfortable
They did console themselves
that I am nobody big

I am nobody big
I am not small either

There is a big difference…

The Trail Behind Me

There's a trail from the past behind me
From whence in this moment I arrive
I look forward to see
Where it wants me to strive
The smile on my face
Belongs to those who helped me thrive

The chosen and unchosen soul friends
The given and unchosen of relationships
With their simply Being or coaxing mends
Diffused and dissolved perceived hardships

I have all of You in my heart
To walk with You, I would go back to start
Gratitude for You will keep You forever with me
Especially when I seem to have parted ways with thee
There's times when only You can make me less lonely

That's when I look back at the trail
Find the bend where you found me frail
Then I walk forward steadily a mile
Taking with me the newfound smile

A Lazy Afternoon

Earth, Water, Sunshine
And a lazy afternoon
Are enough for some flowers to bloom.
What needs have I made significant to not be in gloom?

Are Emotional Beings Fools?

Are emotional beings fools?
While all others delightful cools?
Tears on one come more easily
While make the other fidgety

It seems emotionals never
Appreciate general humor
It seems they prefer suffering
As if that's life in buffering

For them the roller coaster's in the mind
Terrified of the amusement park kind
One rides them with eyes and hands open
Other squeezes shut & clenches tight often

Pick on experiences & words said
Take them to that corner of the head
Dissect and digest and juice
Wring it out for what is of use

Simple joy of Being is that for these fools
What an exhilarating high is for the cools
Time again both strive to reach the place
Beyond thought and action, of solace

Fools look up with amazement at cools
Cools look down with amusement at fools
Nodding their heads in nays
About the other's weird ways

But once they sit down to talk together
To their surprise they enjoy each other
As they share their own living adventure
Realize the point of both Inner and Outer

Inner adventures make you alive to life
Outer adventures make you alive at life
It's each of their challenge
To break the walls they make and manage

Do Nothing

Choose to often do Nothing
Choose to not play the game
Choose to simply stay & Be
Choose the seemingly insane

Try it
Do Nothing
For an hour
For a day
For a month

For any length of time
Know what really is the fight
Win over that all in the mind
It is the Brave
Who can truly rest on this planet
Their choices are such…

Just Be
Aware
Then watch
Prowess simply becoming You
None of it you feel the need to be shown
Yet you are seen as powerfully grown

Gerardo Flores

Gerardo Flores is the co-conspirator who gave Jyoti the courage to host regular poetry circles in her home. He dislikes bios and the usual introductions. He loves technology, books, birds, travels, peanut butter, grapes, languages, doodling and poems. He once jumped out of a plane just because he thought he was afraid of doing it. He can sing and dance, and has been known to ask direct questions. His friends consider him the best pal they could ever have. Everyone in our poetry circle loves to hear him read poetry out loud.

Catullus: 101

Multās per gentēs et multa per aequora vectus
        adveniō hās miserās, frāter, ad īnferiās,
ut tē postrēmō dōnārem mūnere mortis
        et mūtam nēquīquam alloquerer cinerem
quandoquidem fortūna mihī tētē abstulit ipsum
        heu miser indignē frāter adēmpte mihī
nunc tamen intereā haec, prīscō quae mōre parentum
        trādita sunt trīstī mūnere ad īnferiās,
accipe frāternō multum mānantia flētū.
        Atque in perpetuum, frāter, avē atque valē.

        Gaius Valerius Catullus
        (c. 84 BC –54 BC)

Many are the terminals and many the border guards I've seen
        To come to this shitty wake, my brother.
To pour one out for you, a last gift;
        Empty words for empty ashes,
When fate already took from me you in your you-ness.
        Fuck. My harshly-taken brother,
Now, in the old ways of old men come before,
        You get a last grim tribute at your wake,
Wet with a brother's many tears.
        And forever after, brother, well met and farewell.

Anuradha Gajaraj-Lopez

Anuradha holds a postgraduate degree in Journalism and Mass Communication. She was a reporter with The Times of India and later a Special Correspondent with The Asian Age national newspaper in India.

Anuradha has authored over 20 books. The series based on the sacred discourses of Agasthiyar Vazhipaadu has found readership worldwide. She lives with her family in Clovis, California.

Find her work on:

Agasthiyar Vazhipaadu
https://www.amazon.com/author/anuradhagajaraj-lopez

Agasthiyar Vazhipaadu (agastyagnanapeetamca.blogspot.com)
https://agastyagnanapeetamca.blogspot.com/

Agathiyar Valipaad - YouTube
https://www.youtube.com/channel/UCEons12UnOcSwSf2XUfxzRw

Devotion

Is there selfishness in devotion?
I pondered.
In the self, knowing itself
There was nothing !

No devotion, no knowledge
No act, no thought
Nothing even to adore!

Gratitude

I am so grateful
For the gift of writing
That has been
bestowed
By the divine on me.

All my yearnings,
All my pain and joy
Flowing through my pen
Have filled pages instead
And left me completely free!

They ask me
What do you yearn for?,
Name? Fame? Riches?
Surely there is
Something you must seek?

Oh! What do I say?
How shall I tell them?
In writing it all down
Desire or pain
No longer belong to me!

Sanyasi

Saffron clothes.
Do not a renunciate make
Not on mountains
Or deep forest
Can he be found!

Look around,
He that in worldly duties
Seemingly intent
Holds no anger,
desire or lust within

He, the true renunciate
having the six traits renounced
Action performs
In God alone
His whole being immersed!

She Stood By Me

Through our travels
and travails
Through many challenges
And terrible pain
Quietly, she stood by me

Through paths known
And unknown
Through trials smooth
Or hard
Uncomplaining, she stood by me

Through laughter
And copious tears
Through sunshine
And lashing rain
With quiet strength, she stood by me

Barely stepping into her teens
While others
Laughed and romped carefree,
Facing the harsh reality of life
Stoically, she stood by me

Not once did she complain
Not once did she cry or weep
She held her head high
And with quiet dignity,
My daughter, she stood by me.

Would I have borne
All this?
Without her quiet strength
And unfailing trust?
Without My daughter,
Who always stood by me!

Navaneet Galagali

Navaneet is a software engineer in the bay area with a fascination for Sanskrit poetry. As a lamp lights another lamp, joy increases when shared. With this in mind, he makes bite-sized English translations of Sanskrit and Kannada literature with the intention to give connoisseurs an experience of the rasa (essence) in a short span of time. In addition to the print version, you can find his creations on his YouTube channel:

https://www.youtube.com/rasaganga

Matrpanchakam

Shankaracharya, whose time can be dated back to the 7th century, is one of the prominent philosophers of India and he's composed a collection of verses on his Mother known as Matrpanchakam. He became an ascetic and left home at an early age so he was separated from his mother. After his mother passed away, he composed these touching verses known as Matrpanchakam. Here's a sample:

(Matrpanchakam by Shankaracharya)

मुक्तामणिस्त्वं नयनं ममेति राजेति जीवेति चिरं सुत त्वम् ।
इत्युक्तवत्यास्तव वाचि मातः ददाम्यहं तण्डुलमेष शुष्कम् ॥

When I was young, you used to call me affectionately like this. "You are my pearl", "You are the apple of my eye" "Raja", "Live long, my son".

O mother, inside your moth that used to call me with such affection, I'm giving in return a handful of dry rice.

Before cremation, as part of the final rites, dry rice is placed in the mouth of the deceased. We can feel his sorrow that for a mother who cared so much for him, in the end, all he's able to offer is a handful of dry rice.

Even an ascetic like Shankaracharya, who has renounced all worldly possessions, yielded before the love of his mother.

On this occasion of Mother's day and Shankara Jayanti, I felt this was an appropriate verse to honor both of them.

Fun banter between Krishna and Satyabhama

(Krishnakarnamrtam by Leelashuka)

अङ्गुल्या कः कवाटं प्रहरति कुटिले माधवः किं वसन्तः
नो चक्री किं कुलालो नहि धरणिधरः किं द्विजिह्वः फणीन्द्रः ।
नाहं घोराहिमर्दी किमुत खगपतिः नो हरिः किं कपीन्द्रः
इत्येवं सत्यभामाप्रतिजितवचनः पातु वश्चक्रपाणिः ॥

Satyabhama is one of Krishna's wives. One day, she's upset because Krishna was visiting one of his other wives. So when he returns and knocks on the door, she pretends like she doesn't know who it is.

She asks:

अङ्गुल्या कः कवाटं प्रहरति - Who goes there, tapping at the door?

So Krishna replies,

कुटिले माधवः - My playful lady, it is I, Madhava (which is one of Krishna's names).

So she asks:

किं वसन्तः? - माधवः also means the spring season. So she asks, is it spring? She's not letting up that easy.

He responds:

नो चक्री - No, I am the one who wields the chakra (the discus).

किं कुलालो? - Oh are you a potter? Potters also use a wheel to shape their clay. Are you one of those?

Krishna plays along.

नहि धरणिधरः - No no, I'm just the person who sustains the entire world. Krishna is an incarnation of Vishnu after all.

But Satyabhama's not impressed.

किं द्विजिह्वः फणीन्द्रः? - Oh are you that snake with two tongues that supports the world on its hoods? She's referring to Adishesha. Notice the word द्विजिह्वः - snakes have two tongues, and so do liars. So she's hinting something here.

Krishna responds.

नाहं घोराहिमर्दी - No I am the killer of snakes. He's still trying to come out on top.

किमुत खगपतिः? - Oh so you're Garuda, a bird. She's not having it.

Krishna tries a different tactic.

नो हरिः - No, I'm just Hari, very simple.

Unfortunately for him, the word 'Hari' also means monkey in Sanskrit. So she says:

किं कपीन्द्रः? - Oh so you're a monkey'.

Finally Krishna gives in and accepts his defeat - which I suppose married men can relate to.

The verse however, ends with a benediction.

इत्येवं सत्यभामाप्रतिजितवचनः पातु वश्चक्रपाणिः - May he who has been defeated by Satyabhama protect us all.

Bhagavad Gita

"Now I am become Death, destroyer of worlds."
Oppenheimer quotes this line from the Bhagavad Gita."
Verse 32 from Chapter 11.

On July 16th, 1945, Oppenheimer and his team of scientists successfully test the atomic bomb, and Oppenheimer remembers this line.

The Bhagavad Gita is a dialogue between Arjuna, a warrior and Krishna, his charioteer. A war is about to take place, and Arjuna is conflicted. He's not sure what to do. And so a philosophical dialogue takes place between him and Krishna. In the 11th chapter, Krishna reveals his cosmic form, showing the evolution and dissolution of worlds. And Arjuna is overwhelmed by awe and fear and he asks who are you, what are you? And Krishna responds. This verse, the one that Oppenheimer quoted, is his response.

(Bhagavad Gita)

कालोऽस्मि लोकक्षयकृत्प्रवृद्धो लोकान्समाहर्तुमिह प्रवृत्तः ।
ऋतेऽपि त्वां न भविष्यन्ति सर्वे येऽवस्थिताः प्रत्यनीकेषु योधाः ॥

I am Time. Oppenheimer translates this as Death, but it's more than that.

I am Time, engaged in the dissolution of worlds—लोकक्षयकृत्प्रवृद्धो

And even without you—ऋतेऽपि त्वां! येऽवस्थिताः योधा

All these warriors you see, सर्वे न भविष्यन्ति—They will cease to exist. They are all already in the clutches of Time.

So that's the original verse. It seems Oppenheimer was reminded of this verse and its imagery of the dissolution of worlds after witnessing the destructive power of the nuclear weapon he had helped create.

Hanuman Jayanti

Today is Hanuman Jayanti, where we celebrate the birth of Hanuman. We're familiar with his noble qualities - his courage, his strength, his steadfast nature, his friendship with Rama, his devotion towards Rama, his courteous conduct. To add to all of that, I want to highlight an episode from the Valmiki Ramayana which shows his playful nature as well.

Hanuman has gone to Lanka to search for Sita. At night, he secretly enters Ravana's inner chamber and sees Ravana lying asleep with the women of his harem sprawled around him. Away from all of them, on a separate bed, he sees Ravana's young wife Mandodari wearing ornaments and sleeping peacefully and mistakes her for Sita. He's overjoyed because he thinks he's found Sita and he does a little victory dance Maharishi Valmiki has been kind enough to record for us.

(Valmiki Ramayana)

आस्फोटयामास चुचुम्ब पुच्छं ननन्द चिक्रीड जगौ जगाम ।
स्तम्भानरोहन्निपपात भूमौ निदर्शयन् स्वां प्रकृतिं कपीनाम् ॥

He leaps into the air and kisses his tail. He rejoices and sings, presumably quietly so as not to wake up the others. He climbs up pillars and jumps down to the floor, showing his playful monkey nature.

After he calms down, he thinks about it, and he realizes that Sita wouldn't be wearing all these ornaments and sleeping so peacefully in Ravana's inner chamber. She must be somebody else.

अन्येयमिति निश्चित्य भूयस्तत्र चचार सः So he continues his search for Sita and he ends up finding her in the Ashoka vana.

So as we bring to mind Hanuman, his courage, strength and wisdom, let us also remember his playfulness and jovial nature. Wish you all a Happy Hanuman Jayanti.

Ganga Lahari

Here's a verse from Ganga Lahari by Jagannatha Pandita, which was translated into Kannada by Pandharinathacharya Galagali.

(Ganga Lahari, Kannada translation)

ಗಾಳಿ ಲೀಲೆ ಲೋಲಲೆಯ ಲಹರಿಯುಯ್ಯಾಲೆ ಲಾಲಿ ಲುಲಿತ
ಕಮಲ ಗಲಿತ ಕಿಂಜಲ್ಕ ಮಿಲಿತ ಕುಂಕುಮದ ಕಾಂತಿ ಕಲಿತ |
ಇಂದ್ರನೂರ ಸುಂದರಿಯವೃಂದ ಎದೆಗಂಧಚಂದನಗರು
ಕೂಡಿ ರಮ್ಯ ರಸರಾಡಿ ಕಳೆಯಲೆಮ್ಮೆಲ್ಲ ಬಾಳಿನೊಗರು ||

The wind is singing a sweet lullaby as it undulates over the Ganga river causing its waves to move back and forth like a swing.

In that wind, lotuses are shaken, and the pollen has fallen loose from the lotus stalks into the river. And the river attains a saffron red shimmer.

From the city of indra, meaning swarga, the beautiful apsaras have sandalwood paste anointed on their bodies. And the Ganga river, which flows across the three realms, has imbibed some of that essence.

May this delightful blend which is the water of Ganga relieve the vagaries of our lives.

Reena Kapoor

Techie turned writer, playwright and photographer, Reena Kapoor grew up all over India as an "army brat". That wandering sensibility is reflected in her debut poetry collection ARRIVALS & DEPARTURES: JOURNEYS IN POEMS

Reena's poetry and stories have appeared in *Bluebird Word*, *433 Magazine*, *Literary Yard*, *Discretionary Love*, *Flash Fiction Forum*, *Ariel Chart*, *Tiny Seed Journal*, *Writing in a Woman's Voice*, and *India Currents*. Four plays by Reena were produced by *EnActe Arts* in 2021; and her latest full length play was selected for *EnActe's* **New Works Festival** in 2023.

Reena's been a **Citizen Historian** with **The 1947 Partition Archive** collecting oral histories from witnesses of India's Partition since 2011.

She graduated with an undergraduate engineering degree from **IIT Delhi** and a Master's from **Northwestern University**. She's worked as a software product professional for 25 years and mentors social enterprises through **Santa Clara University**. She actively blogs at **arrivalsanddepartures.substack.com** and on Instagram at **@1Stardusty**.

She's Gone

Ever so slowly she lets my hand go
I feel her caress my fingers, my palm
I see her vanishing, slipping away
She's all I want, I try to hold on

She whispers I'll be back here soon
Keep the Sun, and life's heart young
Plant those dreams, wait for me
Bask under the sky, stare long at the moon

And like a wisp of fragrance...she is gone
I'm left in a shiver, a longing deep
Still I smile; on her promises I dwell each day
A crisp bright wind carries me along

The fires, they crackle, the lights arrive
Pagan rituals warm up this hearth
I'll await your return, Summer
While with steely resolve, reflect your light

Instructions For When You're Lost

It's possible you'll get lost.
If you do, simply wait for spring.
One day you'll see her prancing outside.
You'll turn away, seeking refuge in your busy-ness.
Instead, step out.
Let the giggly grass, the foolish flowers, the sun's
    snuggly nudge awaken you.
A bird may perch on your shoulder.
You'll want to chase it away.
Instead, let it sing.
Listen, hum.
You'll scold yourself for taking so long to return.
Refuse.
Say, "I found my way back, didn't I?"
Find your reflection in the dew, echo in the garden chimes,
    and poetry in birdsong.
And whisper, "Welcome back!"

Betrayals Of The Sun

What does it feel like for a little child
When a younger sibling arrives too soon?
The world still a wide open prairie refracts
affections, attentions rendering darker
her world in unpredicted shadows

What does it feel like for an arranged bride
to find her husband longing for another?
Chained to her shining jewels, her tentative feet
cross in trembling step over his threshold
wondering if he'll spare her any light

What does it feel like when we find those
we pinned our hopes on can't be ours?
Marked rocks or planets or suns
whose cores came undone,
light eclipsed by treacherous moons

What if we're lost in galactic darkness
when this road assumes the path of totality?
What if we lit a candle of ancient fuel
from wax trapped within the earth
that captured the sun itself eons ago?

The Postman

Even now I sense a gentle flutter,
mild anticipation
at the mailbox,
my earnest sentry that stands
a hollowed out box
of lost connection
affronting the house
in precarious quixotic stance.
Even as these days
colorful papers arrive
to deliver nothing
to tear open and read
No long awaited letters
delivering dreams or love
Reassurances on a postcard
from a traveling friend
Tall claims with pictures of vistas
that fade memories before the ink
No telegram with congratulations
or even a birthday wish!
As if the world ghosted us
before that was even a thing!

Mostly I march arriving sheaf of papers
straight to the recycle bin
I wonder if the mailman watches me
make this rude terminal jaunt
to promptly dump what he delivered
for shredding and pulping this load
however it is they recycle these days,
inventing new uses and wants
Some say recycling does nothing—
they don't even sort the paper from plastic!

Yet I choose to imagine the paper is rebirthed
with loftier ambition, transformed
into kites drifting skyward carrying dreams,
or earthly bags to ferry our loads
or covers for earnest journals we write in
when we tire from punching keyboards
I remember a time our handwriting
an extension of our talents and foibles
was something we self-consciously owned
a hearkening to the days when
our fingers etched in ink and lead
papered spaces for our lonely souls!

Remember the time you and I wrote endless pages,
streams we let flow across the seas
envelopes sealed and delivered by the "postman"
grandly British in his designated title
Sometimes arriving once a month
and if our luck held, maybe twice
yours articulately stamped "By Airmail"
intrepid musafirs[11] on his Hero bicycle
transmitting long accounts of our days apart
so I could know what it was like, as could you
the restless grayness of our hours, faded colors
that only our reunion could paint afresh.
A life together we sketched on those pages,
engraved, entwined; no one divining the hearts enclosed.
So when he arrived on Holi,[12] Diwali[13] for a baksheesh,[14]
I weighed in: his demand is entirely well earned!

---

[11] *musafir*: Urdu for traveler

[12] Holi: Spring festival of colors in India

[13] *Diwali*: Autumn festival of lights in India

[14] baksheesh: Urdu for tip or bonus payment

How we laughed on our wedding day at the telegram
that arrived with a "massage" of love?

Was it the sender's folly, misspelling or
perhaps a diligent postal clerk determined
the "message" demands a robust transcription
for a whole sensation for love?

In these ambitious times, does the mailman yearn
to bring a long awaited transmission?
I wonder as the trees on my street age and sigh
despite gratitude for what came to be
sometimes an ache for those days of letters,
while love still arrives in texts and memes.
Yet surprises do come, but differently:
for a few months it was a mailwoman plying my street
What a curiosity she would have been for the world
of my childhood; lugging mail on a "ladies" bicycle!
Those months she tries hard to befriend Dishoom[15]
who has no use for her delivery routine
"Threat Level 2!" he'd shout to me daily,
forever on his barking guard
Persistently, but in vain,
and as testimony to good intentions,
she'd leave him a cookie or two.
I wondered at her benevolent overtures
Was it her way of trying regretfully
to make some human connection,
knowing the load she must deliver -
that inert pile of paper - couldn't possibly make!

---

[15] *Dishoom*, our 5 year old Labradoodle who lives up to his name, a comical sound effect like a pow/kapow from fight sequences in stereotypical Bollywood films

Speed

Perhaps we try to fill it all up
To have markers showing we really were here
Little intents, moments we hurried through
Hoping speed, sheer grit will burn through the fear

Ground in our steps in a fool's certain march
Leaving shallow footprints, we smugly displayed
Even as we turned, hurried onto new roads
Winds blew, time flooded in, faded them away

Our breathless jottings of all that we saw
Our mad recounting of lists we crossed off
Miles we covered, turned to see if we missed any
Marking meaningless baubles, petty wars

But as we reached our maturing hour
If we were lucky our hands were warm
Only such loves that sustained with us
Had kept pace, walked steadily along

They said you'll not know how happy you turned out to be
And as I sit listening to the chimes that hum with me
I mark the uncounted: great loves, kind forgivers,
    steady rocks, true mirrors,
No other counter, nor currency could this life be measured in…

Smell, Like A Rake For Memories

Smell, like a rake for memories
collecting leaves of seasons past
fragrant reminders of bygone springs.

I pass a woman on the street
carrying notes from a perfume
my mother wore when I
was just five or six or seven.

A single exorbitant one she owned
gifted by a generous brother
whose unhappy life she'd later rue…

A Christian Dior. Transparent, regal
opulence afloat in a white box.
I can't recall which one, but a
jutting luxury, out of place for
those seasons, soils and suns.

She'd sit at her dressing table to face
the length of an eager mirror, rummaging
her sandalwood box of lipsticks
that one day my sister and I employed,
as we wrapped ourselves in her sarees!

Only to be caught red-handed, red-lipped
rushing to erase all evidence of our
misbegotten color adventure, full of
smudged lipstick, contrition and longing
to grow up faster, please! Faster!

Now I rake up the scent of her presence,
a gravity that pulled me to her room—
as soon as she'd sit to commence—
in full enchantment of her beauty rituals.

I place myself behind her to
behold in rapt fascination, steady
preparations for a social occasion,
watching her closely trace colors,
her every action, line, and hue.

I still recall her green saree
and its lustrous brocade border
made her look as if she
rode frothy waves atop an
effulgent, admiring sea, as it
bowed to her green eyes.

The most beautiful woman in the world.
Still is; is that how green became my color?
Still is, that scent— a rake for my memory garden.
Still is! So I buy myself a similar one, so
I can compel her notes on demand…

Damn, Girl!

a white eyelash has sprouted
much to my vain horror
mascara to the rescue
to fake a youthful aura

hair color has been my friend
to hide so much that's now gray
wrinkles, sagging skin, even beards, i'm told
will eventually have their way

often i laugh out loud
when i think about these terrors
happiness is not in question
but what happened to the mirror?

this girl's not going gently
will be battling aging signs
until I am too tired 'coz
this b.s. takes so much time

Words Like Oxygen

Multitudes of languages occupy me
bed-rocked memory of lifetimes past.
So many I've abandoned in poems,
in dialogue, I can't locate anymore.
Jamming thick at my fingertips,
when I write, on my tongue as I speak,
waiting shyly for a quiet to descend
before they'll consent to use.

Whispering like familiar natives,
they hum nearby, then sit by me,
telling me stories that won't be
told in any other routines,
singing me songs that rhyme
only in homegrown vernaculars,
posing questions that could only be
presented in mutual tongues.

I am lived languages, some whole,
some fragments in liminal blood
binding my reveries to my bones,
waiting for a turn to flow.
Errant words bubble to these lips
like oxygen in a corrupted pond,
sustaining natives and prodigals
without punishment or grudge.

Do you know Hindi for sky?
Do you feel how aakash[16] extends
my presence in expansive peace
to magnanimous heavens above?
Can saagar for the seas and oceans
drown you in its enigmatic embrace?
Do you see how vaadi[17] for valley
chaperones life's river from its lap?

Could pūja, ārādhana, upāsana, ibādat...
for worship, impel you on numinous quests?
Or abundant words persuade you to love
Pyaar, mohabbat, ishq, anurag...
I could simply say I love you but you'd recognize it
only if I whispered in every bhasha[18] I contain
Then you'd know it in every colloquial tongue,
every nuance, every insinuation that inhabits my soul.

---

[16] aakash: "sky"
[17] *vaadi/vadi, sometimes spelled wadi (Arabic), means valley.
(note: no fussy distinction between v's and w's in many of these languages)
[18] bhasha means language.

Love's Music In 100 Words

Long ago foraging in the jungle, I heard music playing itself.
The notes flew, mingling with the winds.
One note stayed near, swaying, swirling about my head.
As it flew, I chased it over hills, valleys, gorges.
It stepped into a river. I jumped in.
The river reached the big city. The note climbed out.
I followed. It played on.
Some listened, few nodded, most didn't hear it at all.
Until one man stopped to dance to its music.
The note rested. I touched the man. We fell in love.
It's been many lifetimes.
We're still dancing to that note.

The Past Is A Country I Used To Know

Past, a country I once knew…
Now exiled, I wait outside
unsevered, pinned to
sharp borders, bones and blood,
constructed from its mud.

Still hear its anthem call
in deafening unison
flailing flags of puppet strings
triggers sparking me to
dances I've longed to quit.

No passport lets me in
No visa stamps accepted
No ports, landings arrive
Stray ships yearning shores
retract to time's undertow.

Through impermeable glass
I watch the past go by—
heat, hubris, harshness of
primal youth; regrets from
pursuit of surface shine.

I claw, I push the partition
of pre-dawn dreams in vain
But then, she rises, turns
I'm looking at me saying,
"Stop coming here,"

"You can't recall the maps
you walked, nor chart such
craters, canyons, climbs!"
I withdraw, wait for her
to show me when she comes:

Fences, forts, frontiers I
built with battle weary
hands; borders defied to
land me where I walk now…
I nod in grateful awe!

Another Self-Improvement Quest?

Step out in the morning to catch that early light
Warm soaks to relax your muscles that get tight

Cold showers are the thing to renew your mood
Wine is still alcohol, once declared to be good

Most of it now declared poison, plus too many carbs
Please just order water, even at a bar

Too much of that plain water can also be an issue!
So add electrolytes, minerals, vitamins for a daily rescue

Those drinks with all those goodies have way too much sugar
You lost weight? So what? Your muscle mass is poorer

Coffee is good for you they told us recently
Avoid coffee, honey, so you sleep soundly

Hike outdoors, connect with nature, find solace in the garden
Watch out for mountain lions, lyme-y ticks, sun and dehydration!

Dentist: Be sure to diligently floss every day
Every day, every tooth, few minutes you can spare

Boys n' Gals at the gym: Strength training is the real game
Pull some weight, get strong, aerobic work maybe bit passè

Yoga guru: The best hour you will spend in a day
Stretch and strengthen, get ready to meditate

Oh Meditation app! Darn! I almost forgot
10 minutes mindfulness to banish all thought

Massage therapist: Stretch daily please
5 minutes EACH MUSCLE, gently with ease!

Spa lady: Darling! Do consider botox, ahem!
Seriously, do you even follow a nighttime regimen?!

Heart's Hometown

I remember all the houses
I've lived, dreamt and dreaded in.

New towns and tongues,
new schools and norms.
Friendships trailed
in suspension,
I scrounged for new.
Fresh allies emerged,
fortifications vaporized.

I don't remember
being afraid,
just peering
into new spaces
of unfamiliar multitudes.

I don't remember
being disoriented,
just repeatedly
supplying:
Where're you from?

I don't remember
sorrow at leaving,
just gathering
antidotes for stings
of refusals ahead.

I don't remember
fearing new places,
just discovering
repeatedly—

How to pretend-belong.

Who's to answer
for how I felt?
Those who primed
such journeys
couldn't; for I looked
behind their backs
at their tied hands.

So I soothed
the gritted girl,
built her forts
without gates
showed her how to
live in bated breath
for new displacements.

The Whole Universe Came Visiting

Upon my return it seemed like
the house had gotten rather full.
I unlocked the door to find
everyone and everything there.
Too crowded to put the baggage down
that'd weighed down my getaway.

Sometimes your troubles don't
remember to stay behind.
Mine bought a ticket,
accompanying me uninvited.
I was back with them, all of
my baggage looking askance.

Now here I am with
all of creation contained
in two faded rooms creaking from
the load, held together like I am
even on days when it's too much.
Who's going to sort through this mess?

A little at a time, one step at a time,
as my father would gently suggest.

OK So I start with the worries:
You really have to go! I'll keep the
strategies, the worst-case-scenarios
but no space for ruminations that rush
in endless circles spilling it all.

Here are the clouds that arrive
to reign over my head.
Please blow them away, will you?
I plead the winds from the future.
Is that the sun hiding in the corner?
Let's ferret him out right now,
dust him off. I'll keep him.

The moon is madness I relish.
Leave him be. He keeps me from caring
too much about the ways in which the earth,
gravity follow rules. So many rules.
I ride his freedom of bordering distractions.

Where's my impatience? She runs
like a second skin I can surely lose.
Let me wrap her up deliberately
in a package. So slow it's tiresome.
Exasperated by every second I take
in my glacial purpose to be rid of it.
Rivers, mountains, cliffs and sands stay.

Let me rummage through the rest;
Flowers? Yes! And trees and birds
that wake me daily? Yes, the earth itself,
oceans, planets, faraway suns I'll keep.
Or where would my wonders travel?

I'll keep my curiosity, my exploration,
my curious questions, unanswerable ones
I want to be here for those when they arrive
as I go sorting through this whole house!
Today's the day the whole universe came visiting…

Monica Korde

Monica Korde is the ***Poet Laureate of Belmont*** & founder of PROJECT **POETRY** 360, her signature initiative aimed at promoting poetry through a variety of community engagement programs & public readings for children, youth and adults.

She curates & hosts the monthly series **Virtual Belmont Poetry Night** that features guest poets and an open mic. As part of her collaborations, she has presented her poetry and produced cross-genre work with many Southeast Asian artists from the bay area.

Her poetry has appeared on numerous venues such as KKUP radio, the ***New Verse News***, San Francisco Public Library, ***Speak Poetry*** and others. Originally from India, she now lives in Bay Area, California.

Reasons for Using the Mango as a Symbol again in a Diasporic Poem

because I had yet to write a poem with a mango in it
because how else do I make it easy for you and manifest
    an image of my homeland?
because it is a metaphor of migration, a typical trope
    and you don't need context
because when I pick mangoes at Costco, I still bring them
    close to my face to have a scent of belonging
because I long to see my mother make aamras from scratch
because the canned kesar mango pulp at the Indian grocery store
    is only sugar, citric acid and nostalgia
because I had never taken a selfie with a mango before
because my mom-in-law sent me pictures of green baby mangoes
    bursting forth on a tree she'd given up on
because cutting crescent-moon shaped slices of the mango
    feels like therapy
because eating a mango is a full-body experience
    those mango fibers hugging my teeth, those sticky mango hands
because the naked mango mess is fresh in my mind
because the skin and stone is a singular shade,
    bright marigold, inside and out
because the urdu poet Ghalib once said:
"Aam meethey hon, aur bahot se hon"
because in the land of avocados and home of the brave
I, too, sing America and dream of mangoes.

Where the Flowers Fall

white like the color of his hair—
white like his aging pellucid nails—
white like his set of teeth left on the corner table

the pinwheel patterned flowers rest face down
exactly the way they were found, underneath
    the tree that bore them.
My grandfather holds his flower-borne hand out, brown, and bare

mountain-like, letting the morning mist roll over
and I watch the bright saffron stalk of the flower
caught up in a giddy frisson, petals holding
    still to the cracks on his skin

harking back to the grey bark of the night-flowering jasmine
ethereal and odiferous, churned out of the milky sea:
'Paarinaha Samudrath jaatho va pārijātah'

Who keeps the sacred tree? Who claims the coral blooms?
sad flower! lost in the fragrant myth, pledging its love
to the sun-god wakes up to a familiar touch

frail fingers stretched out into the light,
weathered with long years under the sun, the bumps
on his palm more pronounced now.

They say heaven lies where the tree is planted
or paradise is made where these flowers fall—
earth-bound, at a gentle shake of the tree

a profusion of Pārijāt!
caught by the leaves, the branches, and in mid-air
by my grandfather's hands, life-giving and
    steady— now a cloud of white.

Smita Shekhar Korde

Smita Shekhar Korde, originally from Pune, now residing in Ahmedabad, India, is a poet and multi-genre author. Her work appears in poetry publications, online and in print, and in various magazines as short stories, articles and interviews in both Marathi and Gujarati languages.

She has organized and presented cultural and literary programs as an MC across various platforms, including **All India Radio** (Akashvani), **Doordarshan** television, and social events in her city. She has served as an editor for popular local magazines and a renowned Marathi-language news publication. From 2013 to 2014, she held the position of education secretary for the **Bhadra Maharashtra Samaj**. She is passionate about social work and has devoted several years recording books, teaching & reading for visually impaired students at various schools.

Her debut poetry collection, AKASHAPALYADCHA AKASH (A SKY BEYOND THE SKY) was published in 2018. Most recently, in 2024, her poetry earned second place in a competition organized by the **Vaidarbhiya Writers Institute "Abhivyakti"** in Nagpur.

Follow her on her YouTube channel
'Shabdashree'
https://www.youtube.com/@shabdashree393

प्रेम म्हणजे ?

कुणास ठाऊक प्रेम
 म्हणजे काय असतं ?
हसता हसता हृदयावर
झेललेले घाव असतं ?
झोकून देऊन पायघड्या
घालून दिलेलं स्वतःचं
आयुष्य असतं ?
की नकळत उचललेल्या
बऱ्या वाईटाच्या
जबाबदारीचं ओझं असतं ?
तुझ्या माझ्यातली सीमारेषा
अलगद पुसून एकमेकांच्या
बहरण्याची आस असतं ?
स्वतःच आयुष्य आनंदें
भिरकावून दगडासारखं ठाम राहून
तुला उडायला दिलेलं अवकाश असतं ?
की चुका दाखवून टोचून
छिन्न भिन्न करणारं बाण असतं ?
काय असतं प्रेम म्हणजे ?
तुलाच अवघं जग समजून
तुझ्या कुशीत शिरणारं
निरागस कोकरू असतं ?
की तुझ्या चेह-यावर
मंद स्मित तेवत ठेवणारं
एक शालीन समई असतं ?
रातराणीच्या सुगंधाने वेडावणारं धुंदावणार
आलापांच गान असतं की सागराच्या लाटांची
अव्याहत गाज असतं ?

काय असतं प्रेम म्हणजे ?
मणामणांच्या बेड्या घालून
कोलूत गरगर फिरवणारं
अंदमानचं काळं पाणी असतं
की आपल्या पिल्लांसाठी
शरीर विकून त्यांमुखी
घालणारं घास असतं ?
की स्वार्थ निःस्वार्थाच्या सीमेवर
रेंगाळणारं देहाचं गुलाम
होणं असतं ?
की सहस्त्र योजनं दूर राहूनही
प्रियाचा बनलेला श्वास असतं ?
सुरकुतलेल्या देहाने
तू आधी की मी आधी ची
वाट पहाणं असतं की
साऱ्यांची दूषणं झेलायला
सामोरी तोललेली
ढाल असतं ?

अनंत अथांग असीम अपरिमित
मुक्त 'मी' ला
अव्यक्त 'मी' चं कडकडून भेटवणं असतं ?
काय असतं प्रेम म्हणजे...?

स्मिता शेखर कोरडे

Vaishali Kulkarni

Vaishali Kulkarni is a qualified Pharma professional working in medicine and healthcare industry for about 20 years. She is from Maharashtra, India and has immense love for her mother tongue Marathi. Her love towards Marathi gets expressed through her poetry. Though she covers variety of topics in her writing, many of her poems talk about human feelings and relationships and nature. She has created multiple arts of poetry in collaboration with Varsha More under the hash tag *#chitrolivarshalichya* wherein the words by Vaishali and pictures by Varsha complement each other.

१.

सखा:
काय झालं आजकाल ,पहिल्या सारखं लिहीत नाहीस
लालफुल निळं आभाळ,झुळझुळ पाणी रंगवत नाहीस...
संथ संथ वाहतेसं वाटतं ,खळखळ तुझी जाणवत नाही
सागराला भेटायची ओढ,पहिल्यासारखी ओढत नाही?
दु:खात आसू सुखात हसू ,दुथडी भरून वाहत नाहीस
पाहिल्यासारखं का गं सखे,आताशा तू उधाणत नाहीस

सखी:
काही नाही रे माझं मलाच सगळं कळू लागलंय आता
आभाळ, फुल, पाणीबिणी रंगवून दाखवून झालंय जगा
आता माझं माझं चित्र मी, माझ्या पुरतेच रंगवते...
खरे ते रंग हवे ते आकार ,पटतील तसे वापरते...
सुख दु:ख हसणं रडणं सगळं बाकी तसच चाललंय
कशावर हसावं कशावर रडावं कोड थोडसं उलगडतंय...
वही कोरी राहत नाहीच लिहिणे रोज तसेच होतेय
लेखणीशी जुळली नाळ आणखी थोडी घट्ट होतेय
आताशा ना आधीसारखी फारशी गर्दीत जात नसते
कवितेला माझ्या ना मी चार चौघात वाचत नसते
भेटलेच कुणी सच्चे दर्दी तर मात्र मैफिल रंगते..
अंतरीच्या तारा जुळतात अक्षर धून ती झंकारते ,
प्रतियोगिता स्पर्धा बिर्धा साऱ्या मग मागे पडतात
समविचारी देवघेव, सच्ची कविसम्मेलने भरतात
उधाण निवळून स्थैर्य ,खळखळाटाला खोली येतेय
काळजी चे कारण नाही रे सखी थोडी मोठी होतेय

जीवनाचा रंगमंच

जीवनाच्या रंगमंची चाले प्रयोग अहोरात्र
कलाकार जरी एक तरी भूमिका अनेक मात्र

रंगविशी तू स्वतःला जशी वेळ जसे पात्र
अभिनयात दंगलेत कुणी शत्रू कुणी मित्र

जनमा येता पहिली घंटा पडली होती कानावर
दुसरी तिसरी आणि मागून येई येई तो भानावर

क्षणात नांदी नाटक सुरु सरसर गेला पडदा वर
बालपणी चा अंक रंगला तरल तरंगे मंचावर

दुसऱ्या अंकी नाटक आले आयुष्याच्या मध्यावर
कितीक पात्रे किती मुखवटे तारुण्याच्या वळणावर

जाळून जीवा कलाप्रदर्शन मिळो टाळी या आशेवर
पणास लावून अभिनय सारा भिनले नाटक अंगावर

आयुष्याच्या संध्याकाळी तिसऱ्या अंका प्रारंभ
रंगकर्मी ते काही गळाले कुणा नव्याने आरंभ

कर्ती करवती रंगदेवता घडवी ऐसा रंग प्रपंच
अखेर पडदा पडण्यापूर्वी त्रिवार वंदीन रंगमंच

बदल...

बदलतेय मी रोज कणा कणा नी
जुने थर चढले काही गळून पडतायत क्षणा क्षणानी
रोज जाणवतय मलाच माझं विझल्या दिवसा अंती
काही वलय नवी रोज गोळा होतायत भोवती...

आजची मी वेगळी आहे कालच्या माझ्या पेक्षा
कधी कालची मी सरस आजच्या आगतिक माझ्यापेक्षा
कधी आजची मी तेजस्वी अनुभवाने कालच्या नवखीपेक्षा

शांत निवांत क्षणी एखाद्या आठवणीचा उघडून कप्पा
कालच्या "मी"च्या आजच्या माझ्याशी होतात मनस्वी गप्पा
घडत जाते नकळत..उद्याची मी..खूप आगळी माझ्याचपेक्षा...कालच्या आणि आजच्याही...

Lalit Kumar

Lalit Kumar writes a regular column in *India Currents Magazine* sharing his passion for adventure and travel. His first book *Years Spent: Exploring Poetry in Adventure, Life and Love* was among top 3 selects in *Indie Spotlight* poetry genre by *BookLife/Publishers Weekly*. His latest book *Yosemite of my Heart: Poems of Adventure in California* was released at San Francisco Writers Conference, Feb '24. Find him on:

Instagram @lalitk06 *or* www.lalitkumaronline.com

Belongings

A book, my phone, a diary, a tablet
Seems I lie scattered all over my room.
I am breathing, I am alive,
and there is a part of me in my things around.

I live in my time, in my body
I desire, I lust, I talk, I laugh.
But I go to work too, day in and day out.
And come back to my things every night.

You see my things keep me anchored.
My mind is ablaze with searing thoughts,
my heart desires a peaceful voyage
and my soul burns with passion, a dozen.
I shift and turn as the changes in the season.
They say I am not a constant in this house, anymore.

You see, with time,
I grew up, but my things did not.
I love them still but where is my heart?
My heart lay nestled in the frontiers
that might be just beyond my room here,
the wide world beckons.

The Second Mountain

Driven, ambitious and passionate,
he had ascended the mountain peak.
Striving relentlessly, with a singular obsession
to climb, to strive and to reach the top.

The panorama was striking from his vantage point.
He felt like the conqueror who defeated all
the wave of happiness swept like the breeze,
invincible he felt; superior he thought in his mind.

As the breeze calmed down, he felt an eerie silence.
Loneliness gnawed at his heart;
the emptiness echoed in his viscera.
'What was the point of it all?' He thought to himself.
His singular achievement meant so little to others.

Contemplating to himself, he narrowed his gaze
and saw the second mountain across the valley.
And lo and behold, it was teeming with people all around.
He hurriedly climbed down and trekked across the valley.

As he approached nearer, he saw people helping each other
ascend the mountain.
Together they climbed and took the tumble together,
negotiating the sharp bends on the way.
He soon realized it's not what you achieve individually
but joy is in how you give away your energy
 in the pursuit of affecting a positive change.

Joy is in helping, in giving, in supporting.
The Cause that deeply moves you
and making it larger than
just your individual self.

So, climb the first mountain, if you must.
To check your fitness on the way ...
But remember, it's the second mountain,
where your impact will pave the others' way.

At the Crossroads

Beads of moments
plucked from the necklace of time,
adrift on the ocean
of my memory;
like a plectrum
pulls upon my heartstrings
rendering it vibrant,
sonorous of the times gone by.

Can I leave those
resplendent moments behind
and walk on?

Kurt Lovelace

An editor, writer, translator, and mathematician, Kurt's work has appeared in *The Lascaux Review*, *North Dakota Quarterly*, *San Antonio Review*, U.K. Lancaster University's *Red Ogre Review*, U.H. Honor College's *Athena* and other journals.

HALFWAY BETWEEN EVERYWHERE is Kurt's most recent collection of poetry, which includes selected translations and essays on poetry. An audiobook is also available.

Kurt has new work soon to appear in *Axon: Creative Explorations*, an international peer-reviewed journal that focuses on the characteristics of creativity and the creative process; and poems in the upcoming Australian anthology, **RICOCHET**, will be out in the Spring of 2025. He has two full length poetry collections forthcoming, **APOPHRADES & INTREPITUDES**, and a third book, **DISFIGUREMENTS**.

Included here are the poems, Παρουσία (*Visitation*) written in Greek, and **Traversé** (*Crossed*) written in French, with their English translations along with Etiquette, Trying to Navigate in Istanbul, and Au Cas où vous Obtiendriez cette Note à Temps, along with Fabulae, translated from the original Latin text. These and others will appear in **POLYGLOT**—a book of experimental multilingual and "mixed language" poems—exploring linguistic cultural communication and miscommunication around the world, forthcoming in the Fall of 2025.

Παρουσία

Να επισκεφθείτε ένα ελληνικό χωριό χωρίς να επισκεφθείτε
ένα ελληνικό χωριό δεν είναι το ίδιο με την επίσκεψη
ένα ελληνικό χωριό. Google Earth όσο θέλετε.
Ποτέ δεν θα δοκιμάσετε τον καφέ. Ποτέ δεν θα μυρίσετε

τα σκατά. Ούτε θα ξαπλώσετε στο άβολο στρώμα
που είναι γεμάτο κοριούς. Δεν θα γίνετε μάρτυρες του αργού σάλιου
που στάζει από τα φθαρμένα χείλη του αλμυρού πανδοχέα
δίπλα στο τζάκι, σκυμμένος με τα γυαλιά του, μουρμουρίζοντας

Ελληνικά.

Visitation

Visiting a Greek village without ever visiting
a Greek village is not the same as visiting
a Greek village. Google Earth all you want.
You will never taste the coffee nor smell

the shit, the uncomfortable mattress
tossing with bed bugs, the saliva crusting lip
of the salty caretaker tindering
the fireplace, bent over in his spectacles, muttering

Greek.

Traversé

Avant même d'être cloué sur la croix
un arbre devait d'abord mourir. Il n'y a aucun doute

qu'il était vivant avant que les clous ne s'y enfoncent.
Un sang inhumain suintait de son phloème rompu.

Puis les Romains ont donné au grand verticille de l'arbre,
sous les pieds pendants, d'une riche flaque

de rouge à l'endroit où les clous ont traversé les os de la cheville,
lui donnant un oeil infectieux, incarnadin,

comme celui de Jupiter. Et l'homme, déjà étalé,
chevauchait le squelette d'os de l'arbre, l'arbre

qui aspirait encore cette eau rouge, riche en fer, dégoulinant
souffrance.

Crossed

Even before he was nailed to the cross
a tree had to die first. There's no question

it was alive before nails drove into it.
Inhuman blood oozed from its punctured phloem.

Then the Romans gifted the tree's large whorl,
below the dangling feet, with a rich pool

of rouge, where the nail went in though the ankle bones,
giving it an infectious eye, incarnadine,

like Jupiter's. And the man, already splayed out,
rode atop the tree's skeleton, its splintered bones

still sucking towards the red, iron-rich water, dripping
suffering.

Au Cas où vous Obtiendriez cette Note à Temps

A l'heure qu'il est, vous avez déjà mangé
la succulente pêche froide
que j'avais rangée au fond du frigo,

dont vous avez probablement pensé
que je gardais
pour mon petit déjeuner.

Pardonnez-moi. Il ne fait aucun doute que votre bouche
l'a trouvé délectable, léchant des lèvres humides
si douces et si

empoisonnées.

In Case You get this Note in Time

By now you've eaten
the cold succulent peach
I'd stashed back of the frig,

of which you probably
thought I was saving
for my breakfast.

Forgive me. No doubt your mouth
found it delectable, licking wet lips
so sweet and so

poisoned

Fabulae

Cura cum quendam fluvium transiret, vidit cretosum lutum, sustulit cogitabunda et coepit fingere hominem. Dum deliberat secum quidnam fecisset, intervenit Iovis; rogat eum Cura, ut ei daret spiritum, quod facile ab Iove impetravit. Cui cum vellet Cura nomen suum imponere, Iovis prohibuit suumque nomen ei dandum esse dixit. Dum de nomine Cura et Iovis disceptarent, surrexit et Tellus suumque nomen ei imponi debere dicebat, quandoquidem corpus suum praebuisset. Sumpserunt Saturnum iudicem; quibus Saturnus aequus videtur iudicasse:

"Tu, Iovis, quoniam spiritum dedisti, animam post mortem accipe; Tellus, quoniam corpus praebuit, corpus recipito. Cura quoniam prima eum finxit, quamdiu vixerit, Cura eum possideat; sed quoniam de nomine eius controversia est, homo vocetur, quoniam ex humo videtur esse factus."

Gaius Iulius Hyginus
(c. 64 BC – AD 17)

Fable

As Care once crossed a certain river, she saw some chalky clay, picked it up, and thoughtfully began to shape it into a figure. As she pondered her work, Jupiter appeared; Care pleaded with him to give it a spirit, and this Jupiter happily bestowed onto it. But when Care wanted her name placed upon it, Jupiter prohibited her, saying that his name must be put on it. As they debated which name it should have, Earth arose and said that it must take Earth's name, since it had provided the body. So, to arbitrate, they invited Saturn to be the judge; whereupon Saturn appears to have judged very equally:

"You, Jupiter, since you gave it spirit, you shall receive its sprit upon death; Earth, since you provided its body, you shall receive its body. And as Care first formed it, Care shall posses it all of the days of its life; but as to the controversy over its name, it shall be called Homo, for it is made out of humus *(earth)*."

İstanbul'da Yön Bulmaya Çalışmak

Trying to Navigate in Istanbul

    It wasn't the streets that where hard but words
Zor olan sokaklar değildi, kelimelerdi.
seslerin eski çimento parke taşlarında
    ancient cemented cobblestones of voices

    and meanings threaded through carpets faded
ve anlamlar solmuş halıların arasından
heceleri şekillendiren dillerin uzun ayakkabılarından.
    from the long foot-wear of tongues shaping syllables.

    Not knowing which way the wind blows,
Rüzgarın hangi yönden estiği umurunda değil.
Durdu ve bana bakıp şöyle dedi:
    I halt a man, and ask the way to Sultanahmet Square?

Amerikan suratını sikeyim.
    I bowed profusely thanking him.

お行儀 | Etiquette

    she lifts up
彼女は箸で寿司を持ち上げる。
       with her chopsticks
            a piece of sushi

    her teeth rip into
彼女の歯は、肉厚のオレンジ色の魚肉を引き裂く。
       thick pulpy orange
            fish flesh

    her fish juice
彼女の魚の汁が私の左目にしみこんで、しみる。
       squirts into
            my left eye, stinging

    the closed slender rose petals
彼女の左手の指は、それぞれ細長いバラの花びらを閉じている。
       of each finger on her left hand
            shields her giggling lips

全てはとても日本人です。

It is all very Japanese.

Yogesh Patel

Yogesh Patel received an MBE for literature in 2020. With many books, film, radio play, and LP records, Patel's poems appear on the **Poetry Wall** of the **Royal Society of Literature** and featured at Cambridge University's Language Library. He runs *Skylark Publications UK*. Extensively published, an award-winning poet, he has also received the **Freedom of the City of London**.

Gestalt Intelligence

Born with skin affirmed,
A citizen, a British passport in hand,

His life, measured by the befuddled standard
A page of the history, unturned.

The upright daffodil bugles the fake spring,
Yet the fool remains unaware; it is still winter!

I could write of the Lady Justice's cold warmth,
A placid face that ensnares, lacking a snug hand.

Three ugly sisters: being, becoming, and belonging,
Have the fourth: betrayal. A bastard no one talks about!!

Yet here I stand, stung by another lost bee—
A drone, an outcast like me, sustenance for the hive.

Oracle

do not blame the wind
for what it drops on my mat
after its agonising migration
I find an autumn leaf
begging me to read its palm

as I possess no such oracle
it turns into a quill

with no offer of words and ink
heartbroken, it takes off
with its transfigured swan

now I stand disappointed
holding my blank paper

begging me for a story

Cataracts

mired in legends and gods
the impatient river rushes
its banks, polluted with temples
seek moxa in an ocean

it harbours the evolution
of blind river dolphins
the buoyant *living fossils*
now experts in side swimming

I can't fathom their optimism-
not in catching silver mahseer or bata
but in glopping through the viscous
sediment humans offer

therefore, I tell my optician
announcing my cataracts:
I have already, happily,
echolocated myself

The river is not of concern
I accept the rainbows of my cataracts
always better than the bannered
blindsided 20/20 vision

Kamala Tyagarajan

Kamala Tyagarajan is a PhD scientist by profession based in the San Francisco Bay Area. She has been passionate about writing poetry for many years. Kamala writes about life and emotions and likes to keep a simple, short style to her poems. She also enjoys writing poetry about biology and chemistry bringing to life the proteins, cells and chemistry she encounters in her scientific work.

Drive

I am driving on life's freeway;
Going along with the flow.
The merges are easy,
Lane changes really difficult
And the exits rare and few;

Good heavens my brakes do not work!!

Roots and Wings

We envy each other,
My friend and I;
I her freedom to fly,
And she that I have bonds that
Hold me to earth...

Bond Energy

One doesn't feel
The strength of the bond
Till tis the time to break
Away:
And there is no choice.

By the Lakeside

Away from the hustle-bustle
And worries of tomorrow;
Questions ebb away,
As silent thoughts hold sway…

Topaz

When settled again, I will look for a four legged friend. 3rd Sutta of Siddhartha is actually based on two true stories—one is Buddha's Fire Sermon, the second is the house fire that occurred on May 8th. The really interesting part is that I had just finished reading the sermon, before falling asleep, and was going to send the sermon to a friend, since he was interested in Buddhism as well. For other poems, stories and essays, please visit:

poeticphonetics.com

Sic Ergo Sum

Retrieving gold from shadows
more than playing fetch—because
truth
as value, does exist
through wisdom built from facts
graphing known and unknown
described as leap of faith
though perhaps mythologies
create parabolic sets
not that truth is relative
(or relations based on fact)
yet calming conscious cortex
seems central to all paths
so sitting on your haunches
ears perked, tongue full of respiration
may just be reptilian brain's
best insight to inspiration

3rd Sutta of Siddhartha
(A True Story)[2]

O Jatilas he began,
how was I to know
that from the pages of the book
enlightenment would flow
the book sat in repose, renewed
twenty something times
until hour appointed
when words illumined mind
he continued,
sense organs, perceptions, feelings
all aflame
and - as if waking to a dream
my life
one and the same
fire, he informed,
finds fuel on which to feed
soul-wise that's called envy,
anger, lust and greed
with cosmic woof and warp
these events aligned
suggesting eightfold path
is related to divine
though wary of my senses,
there was no blessed state
while watching abode burning
midnight on May eight

Sum Ergo Sic

Oculus Dexter, Orbital Sinister
half allegory of the cave
yet, like McDowell in Clockwork Orange
Hetude, you trigger pain
have I implanted morals
to run temporal maze?
is Pavlov sailing wantonly
through IMAXgineered brain?
for every shade of grey,
there is a shade of doubt
yet, tradition everywhere
proves
the truth will out
sometimes back to basics
means just being grounded
listening to a canine friend
whose tale is joy expounded

Vishal Vatnani

Vishal Vatnani lives in San Jose, California and likes to write poetry in English on the topics of love, introspection, social satire, dystopia, and existentialism. He started writing poetry and lyrics at 16 after listening to the song Across the Universe by The Beatles. His literary influence comes from Charles Bukowski. Find him on Instagram @vishalvatnani

The River Walk [Being]

People love the walks of rhythm,
a systematic trance that delivers them from time.
When I look through the eye of the prism,
I see the piecemeal formation of my own mind.

If it had been perfect, it would have been nice,
And similarly the nice would have been perfect.
That dopaminergic niceness with the stealth of mice,
makes me a subject in my own experiment.

The forces were strong from all directions.
They act on me when I stand on your stage.
You confuse my script for knee-jerk reactions.
So you left saying we were on different pages.

But I want to read you an epic,
that I carry in the palm of my hands.
If you zone out, you'll hear me speak of esoteric.
If not, you'll know I was very easy to understand.

It Doesn't Add Up [Becoming]

Standing under the shower head,
the water drenches me in remembrance.
It's not my hallucination, it's my buccal mucosa.
It somehow measures water vapor permeance.

Sublingual thoughts are always linear.
They reverberate in an anechoic chamber.
My sublingual fossa has nice innervations,
more nerves than I could muster in a month.

It doesn't add up, even as I became better at math.

A Snowflake Dining In Texas [Belonging]

Thinking about some tricky problem,
walking down the aisle of makers.
And I make sure I don't slump,
as I pass the old sentinel baker.

I don't want to appear as someone,
looking for someone kind.
Let it be clear that I can't,
always keep you on my mind.

Sitting down on Apple Alley,
a table by the Eggnog plaza.
Right across me is the valley,
where they crucified Jimmy Chen

I don't want to appear as someone,
making up silly rhymes.
They've been worried about it lately,
"Boy, you'll be out of your prime".

Stowing away my pen and paper,
I finally see their eyes.
They were waiting for me to tell her,
If I'd like it with some fries.

I don't want to be somewhere,
where I get to talk but not eat.
Kind lady, she got me crazy,
A quarter pound full of meat.

Sulking my face, somewhat bravely,
I told her that my heart was a see-saw.
Simple plants are all I chew on,
She said, "Oh I'll get you coleslaw!"

Coleslaw, don't make it personal.
But you could be a little bit hotter.
Coleslaw, I just don't care,
But you could get me something better.

No coleslaw for me, please.

www.ingramcontent.com/pod-product-compliance
Lightning Source LLC
Chambersburg PA
CBHW020444090526
44586CB00045B/849